GRAPHIC SCIENCE

A REFRESHING LOOK AT

RENEWABLE ENERGY

WITH

SUPER SCIENTIST

4D An Augmented Reading Science Experience

Summit Free Public Library

by Katherine Krohn | illustrated by Cynthia Martin and Barbara Schulz

Consultant:
Ingrid Kelley
LEED AP, Project Manager
Energy Center of Wisconsin
Madison, Wisconsin

CAPSTONE PRESS
a capstone imprint

Graphic Library is published by Capstone Press,
1710 Roe Crest Drive, North Mankato, Minnesota 56003.
www.capstonepub.com

Library of Congress Cataloging-in-Publication Data is available on the Library of Congress website.

ISBN: 978-1-5435-7248-3 (library binding)
ISBN: 978-1-5435-7544-6 (paperback)
ISBN: 978-1-5435-7252-0 (eBook PDF)

Summary: In graphic novel format, follows the adventures of Max Axiom
as he explains the science behind renewable energy.

Designer	*Cover Colorist*	*Media Researcher*
Alison Thiele	Krista Ward	Wanda Winch
Cover Artist	*Colorist*	*Editor*
Tod G. Smith	Matt Webb	Christopher Harbo

Photo Credits
Capstone Studio: Karon Dubke, 29, back cover;
iStockphoto/Gordo, 25; Shutterstock/Dimyadi Hywit, 10

All internet sites appearing in back matter were available and accurate
when this book was sent to press.

1 Ask an adult to download the app.

 Capstone 4D Education

2 Scan any page with the star.

3 Enjoy your cool stuff!

—— OR ——

Use this password at capstone4D.com

renew.72483

Printed in the United States of America.
PA70

TABLE OF CONTENTS

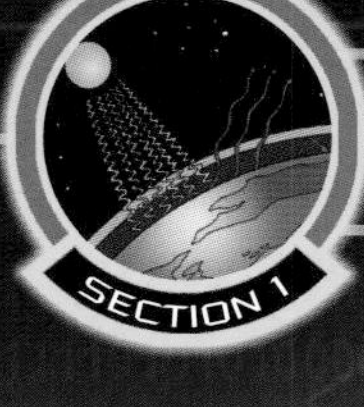
SECTION 1

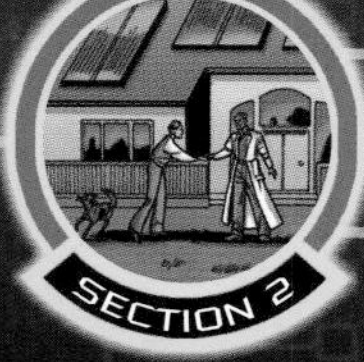
SECTION 2

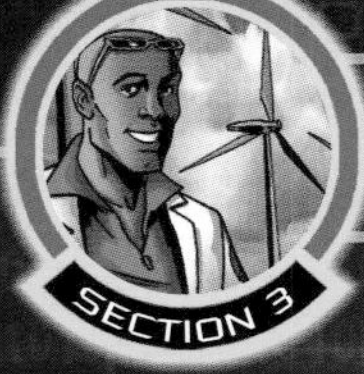
SECTION 3

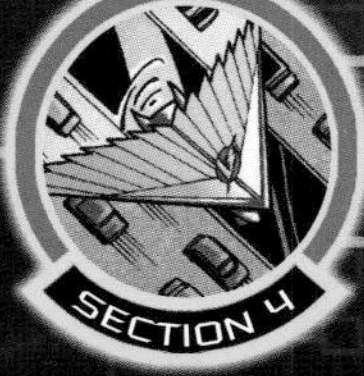
SECTION 4

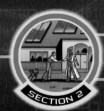

SECTION 1 WHERE DOES ENERGY COME FROM?

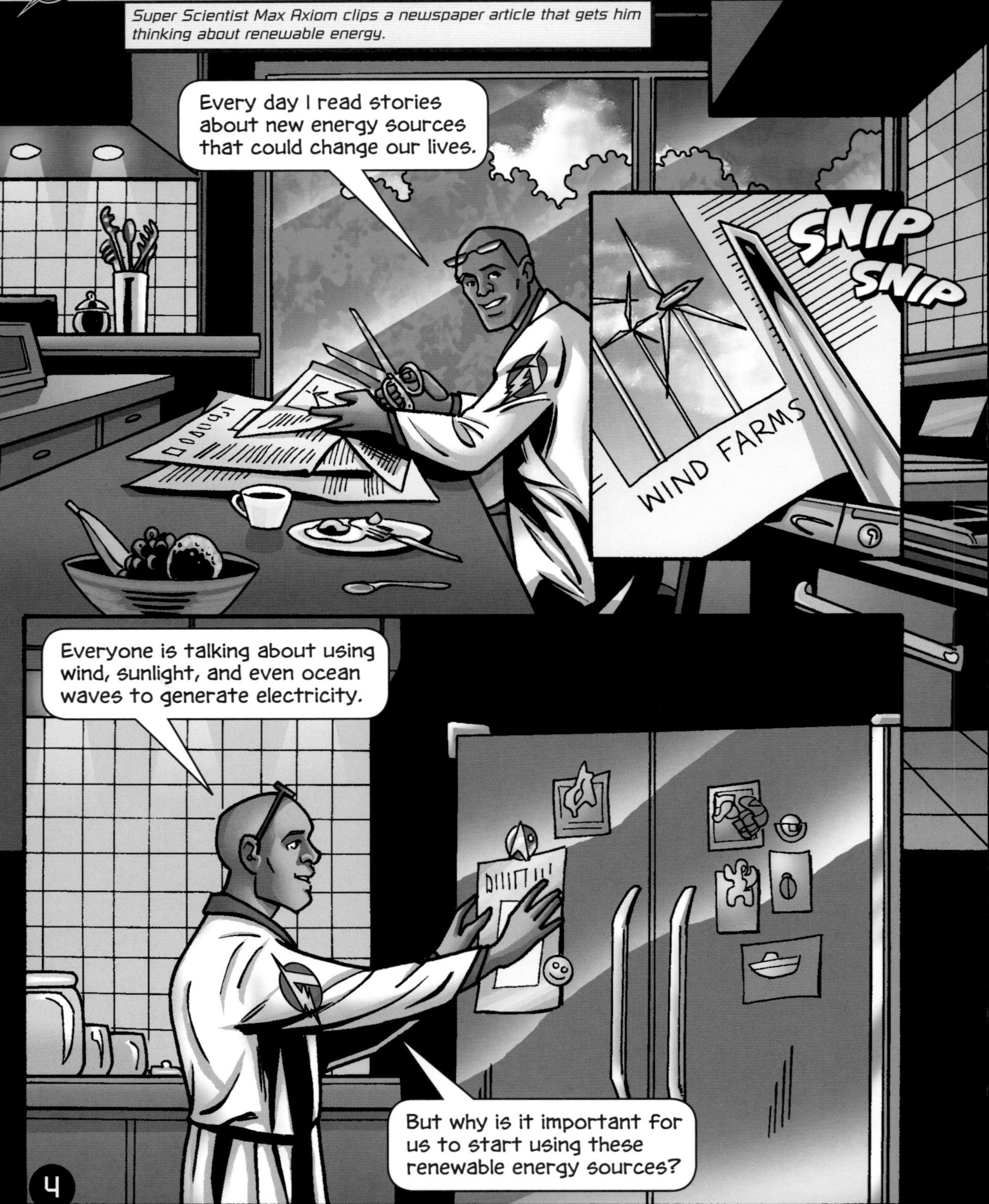
Super Scientist Max Axiom clips a newspaper article that gets him thinking about renewable energy.
Every day I read stories about new energy sources that could change our lives.
SNIP SNIP
WIND FARMS
Everyone is talking about using wind, sunlight, and even ocean waves to generate electricity.
But why is it important for us to start using these renewable energy sources?

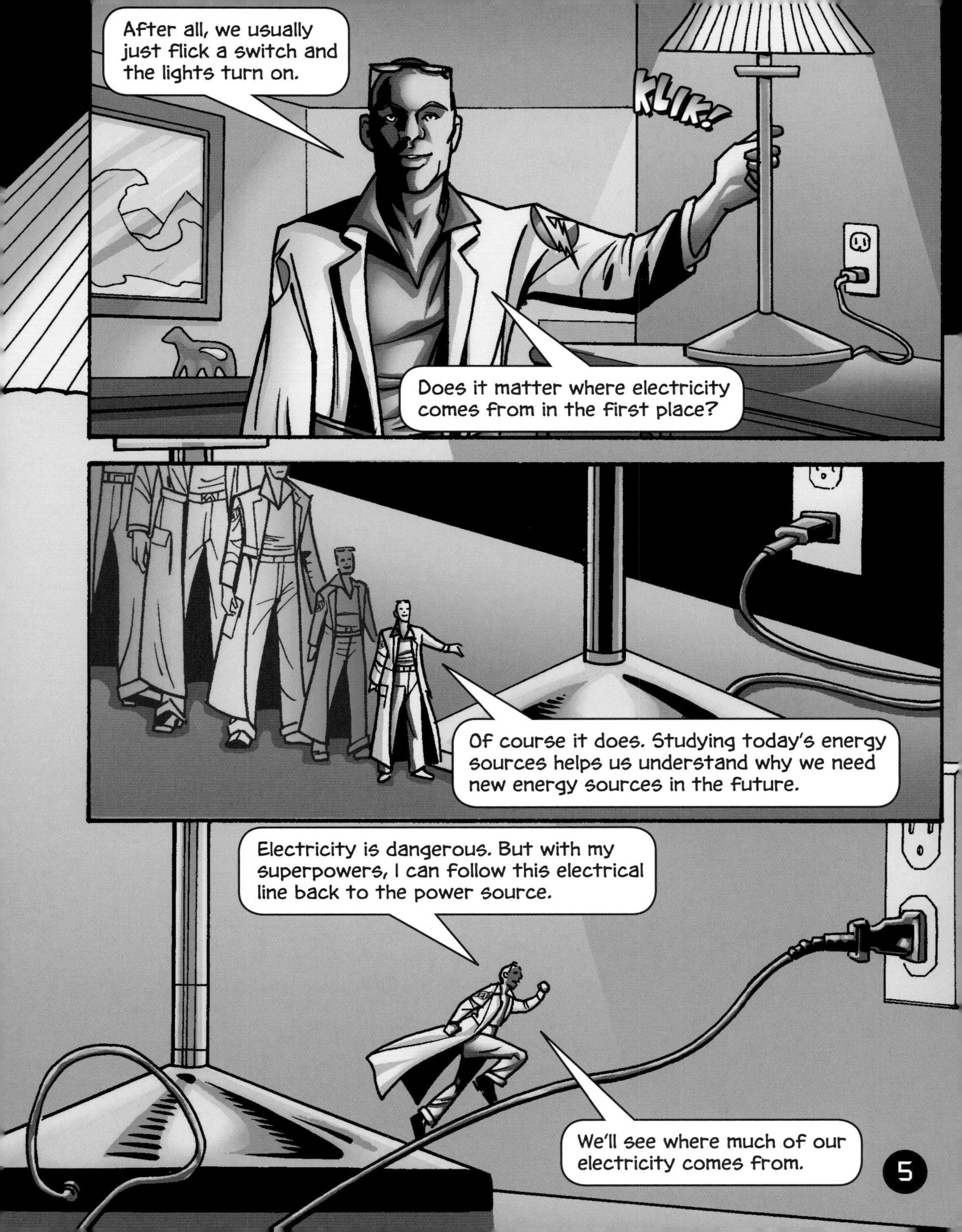
After all, we usually just flick a switch and the lights turn on.
KLIK!
Does it matter where electricity comes from in the first place?
Of course it does. Studying today's energy sources helps us understand why we need new energy sources in the future.
Electricity is dangerous. But with my superpowers, I can follow this electrical line back to the power source.
We'll see where much of our electricity comes from.

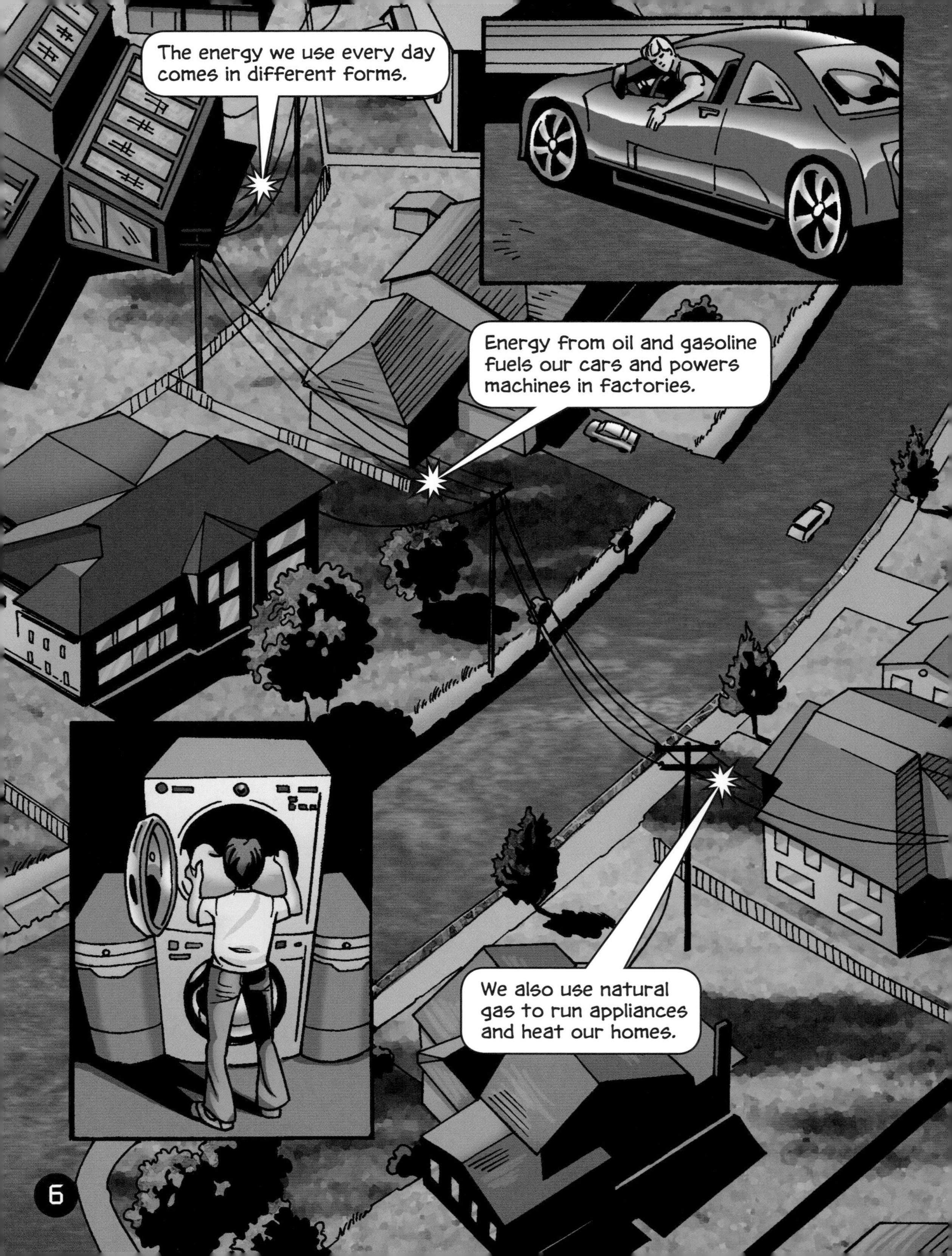
The energy we use every day comes in different forms.
Energy from oil and gasoline fuels our cars and powers machines in factories.
We also use natural gas to run appliances and heat our homes.

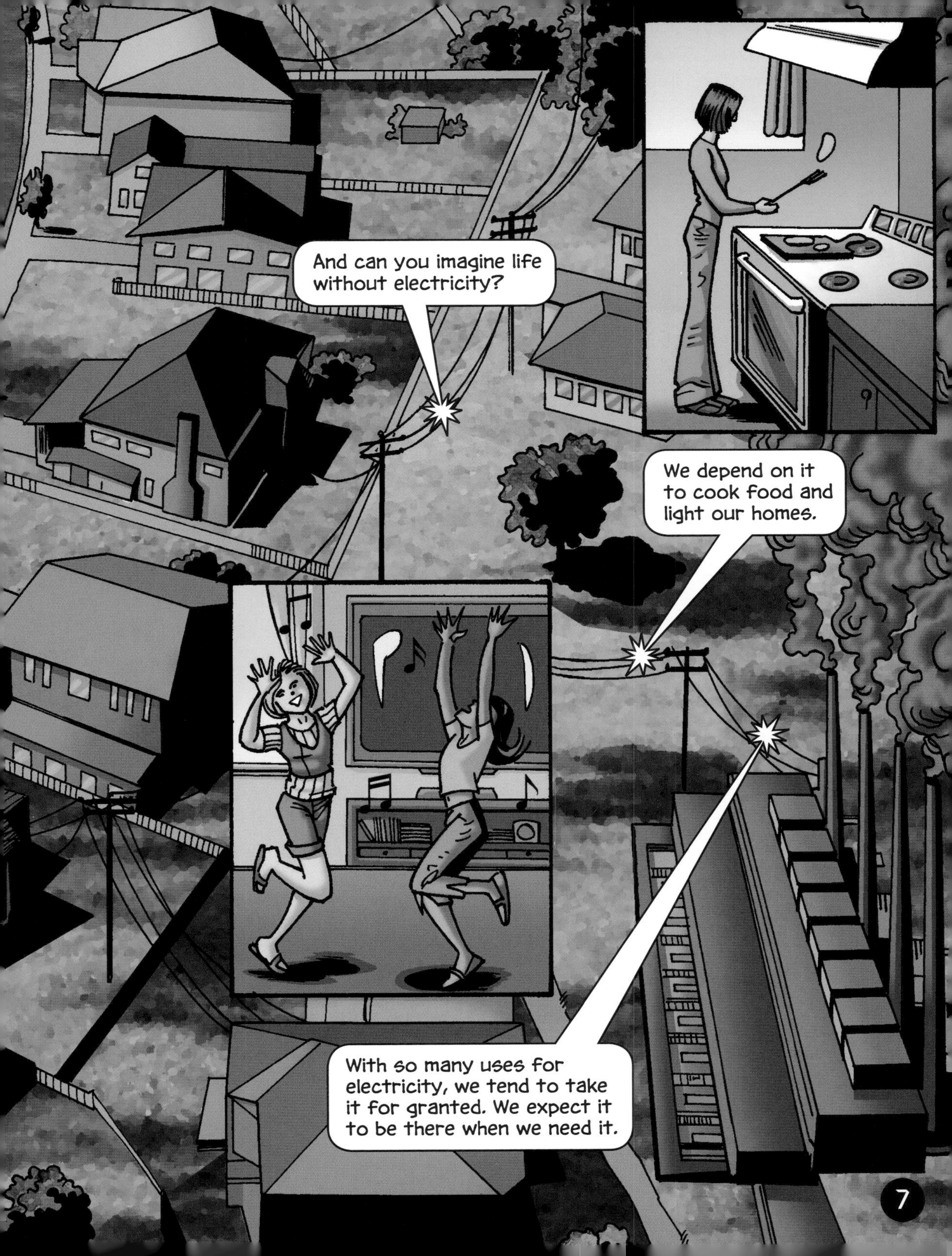
And can you imagine life without electricity?
We depend on it to cook food and light our homes.
With so many uses for electricity, we tend to take it for granted. We expect it to be there when we need it.

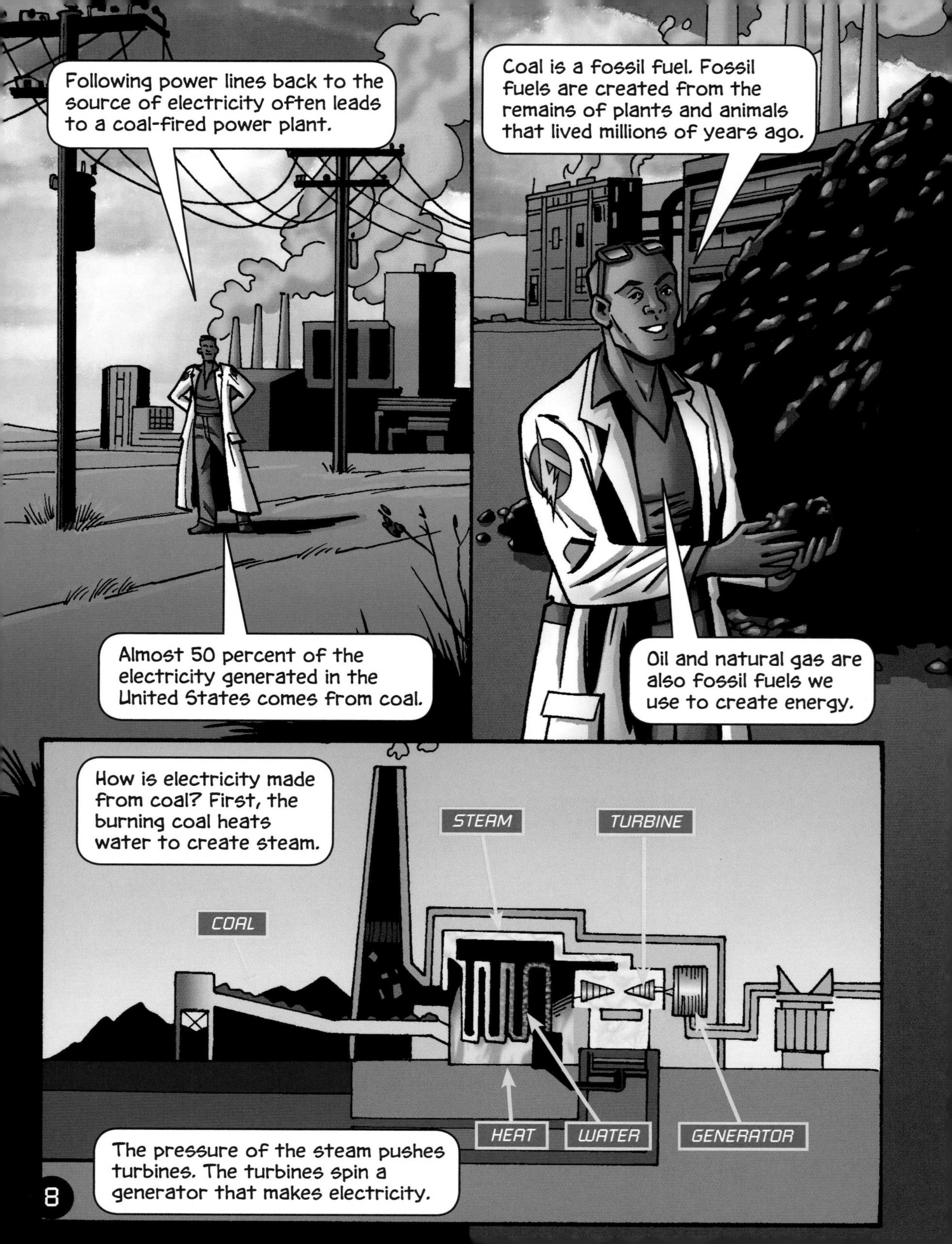
Following power lines back to the source of electricity often leads to a coal-fired power plant.
Almost 50 percent of the electricity generated in the United States comes from coal.
Coal is a fossil fuel. Fossil fuels are created from the remains of plants and animals that lived millions of years ago.
Oil and natural gas are also fossil fuels we use to create energy.
How is electricity made from coal? First, the burning coal heats water to create steam.
STEAM
TURBINE
COAL
HEAT
WATER
GENERATOR
The pressure of the steam pushes turbines. The turbines spin a generator that makes electricity.

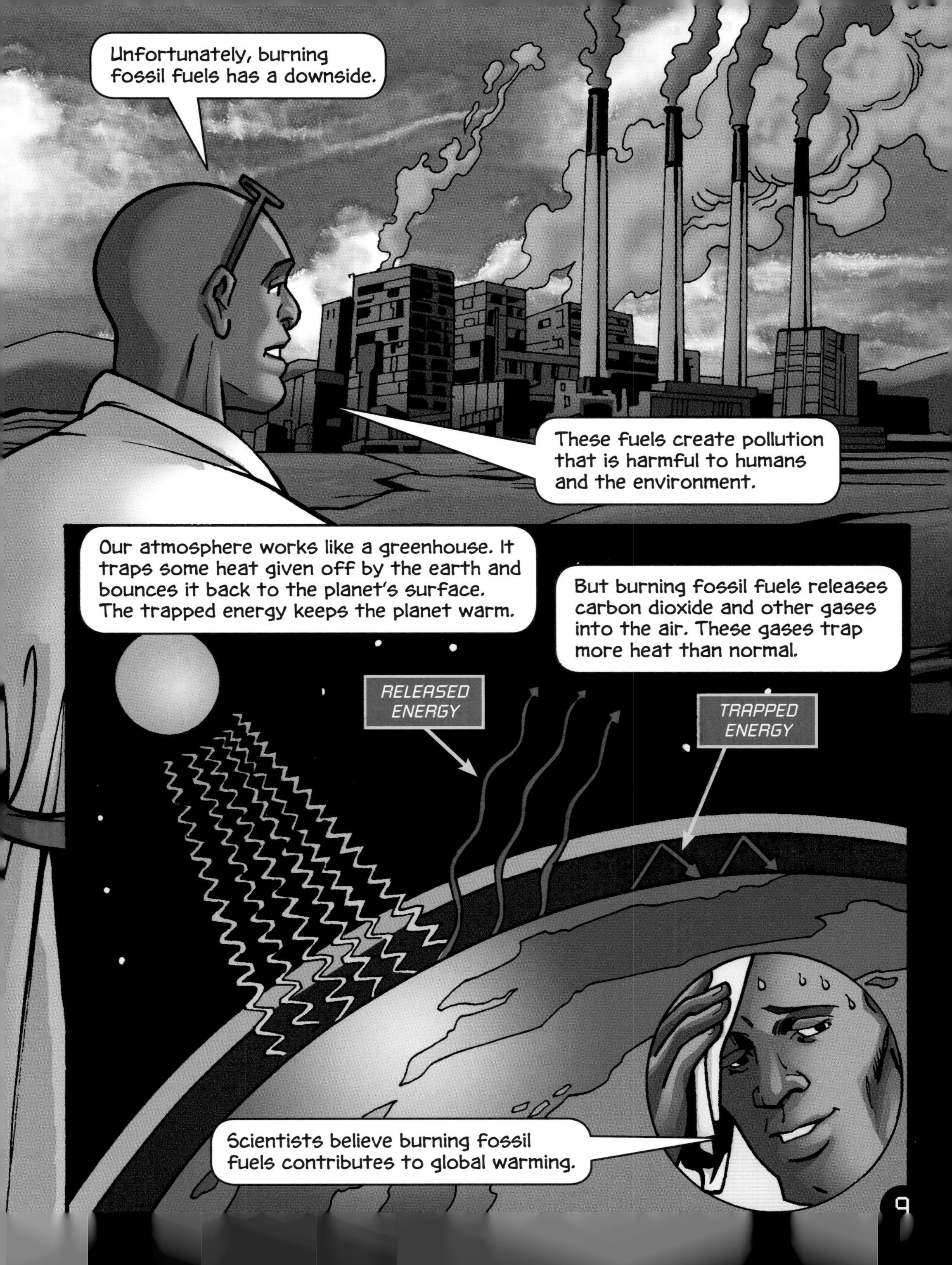
Unfortunately, burning fossil fuels has a downside.
These fuels create pollution that is harmful to humans and the environment.
Our atmosphere works like a greenhouse. It traps some heat given off by the earth and bounces it back to the planet's surface. The trapped energy keeps the planet warm.
But burning fossil fuels releases carbon dioxide and other gases into the air. These gases trap more heat than normal.
RELEASED ENERGY
TRAPPED ENERGY
Scientists believe burning fossil fuels contributes to global warming.

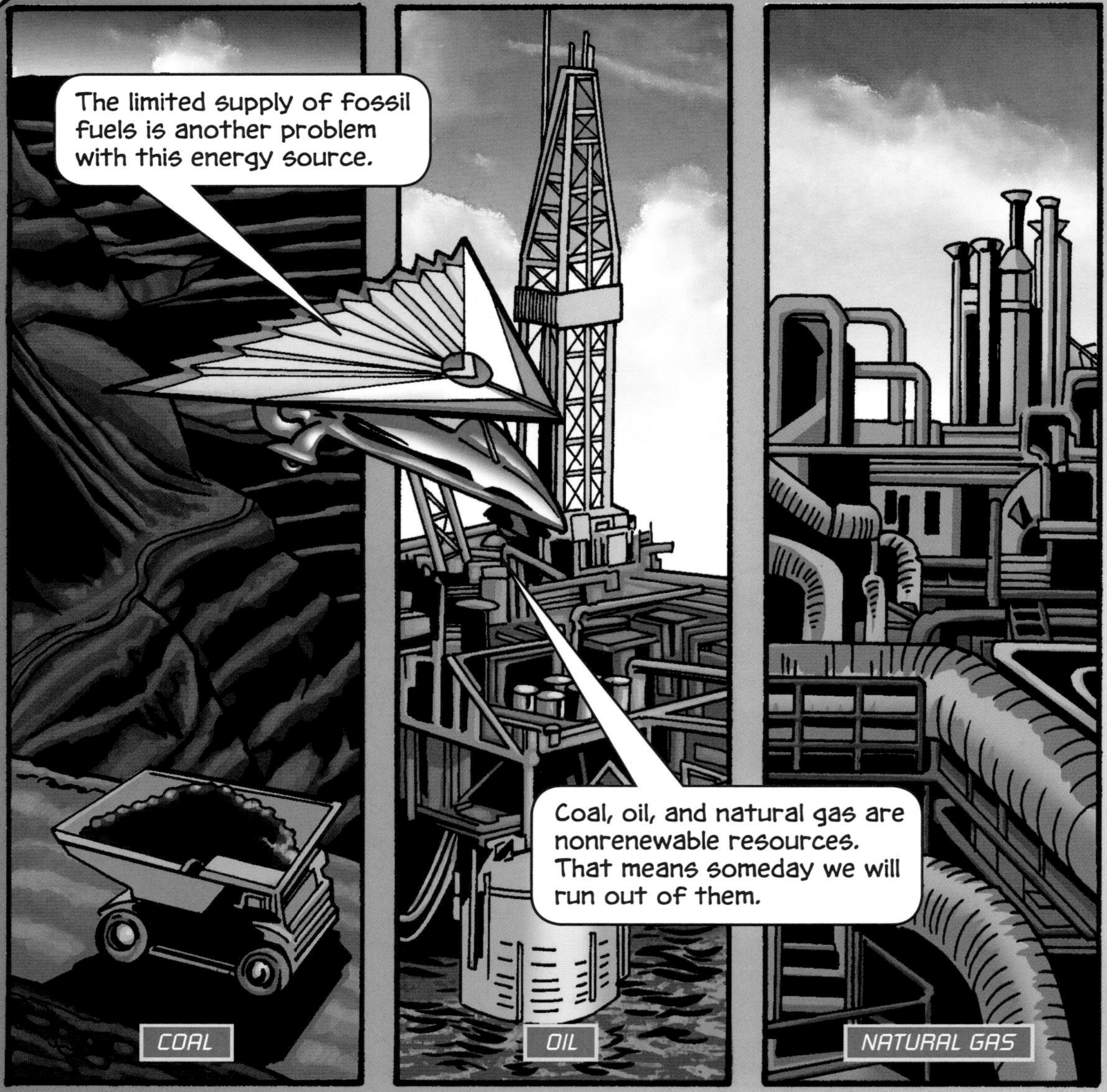
The limited supply of fossil fuels is another problem with this energy source.
Coal, oil, and natural gas are nonrenewable resources. That means someday we will run out of them.
COAL
OIL
NATURAL GAS

CLEAN COAL?

ACCESS GRANTED: MAX AXIOM

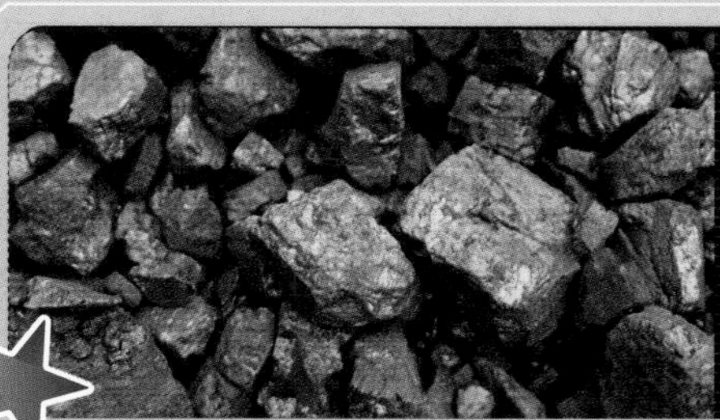

Researchers have developed ways to clean coal by removing pollutants before it is burned. But pollutants like carbon dioxide must be captured and stored to prevent them from being released into the air. Carbon storage technology is still experimental and expensive.

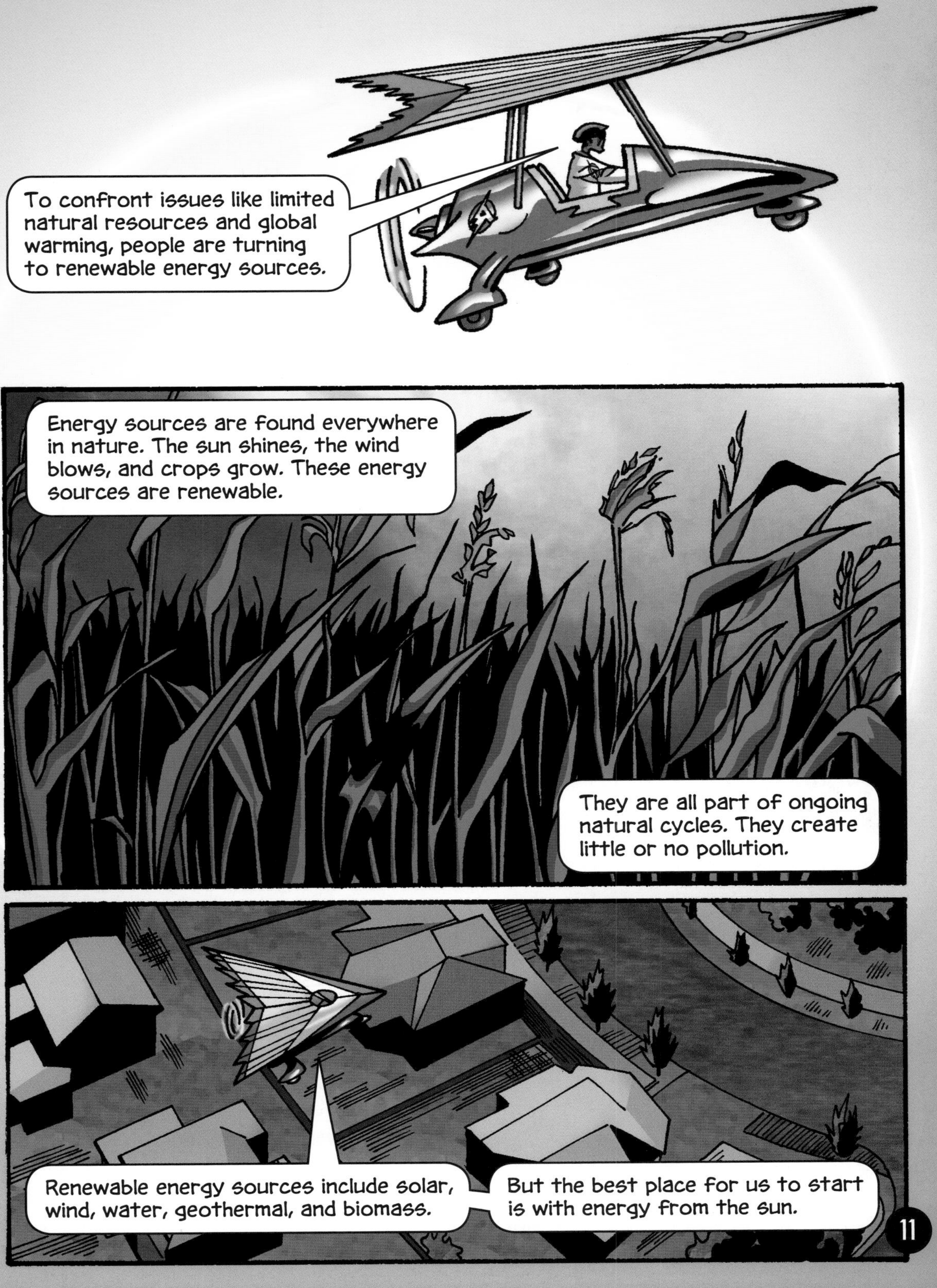
To confront issues like limited natural resources and global warming, people are turning to renewable energy sources.
Energy sources are found everywhere in nature. The sun shines, the wind blows, and crops grow. These energy sources are renewable.
They are all part of ongoing natural cycles. They create little or no pollution.
Renewable energy sources include solar, wind, water, geothermal, and biomass.
But the best place for us to start is with energy from the sun.

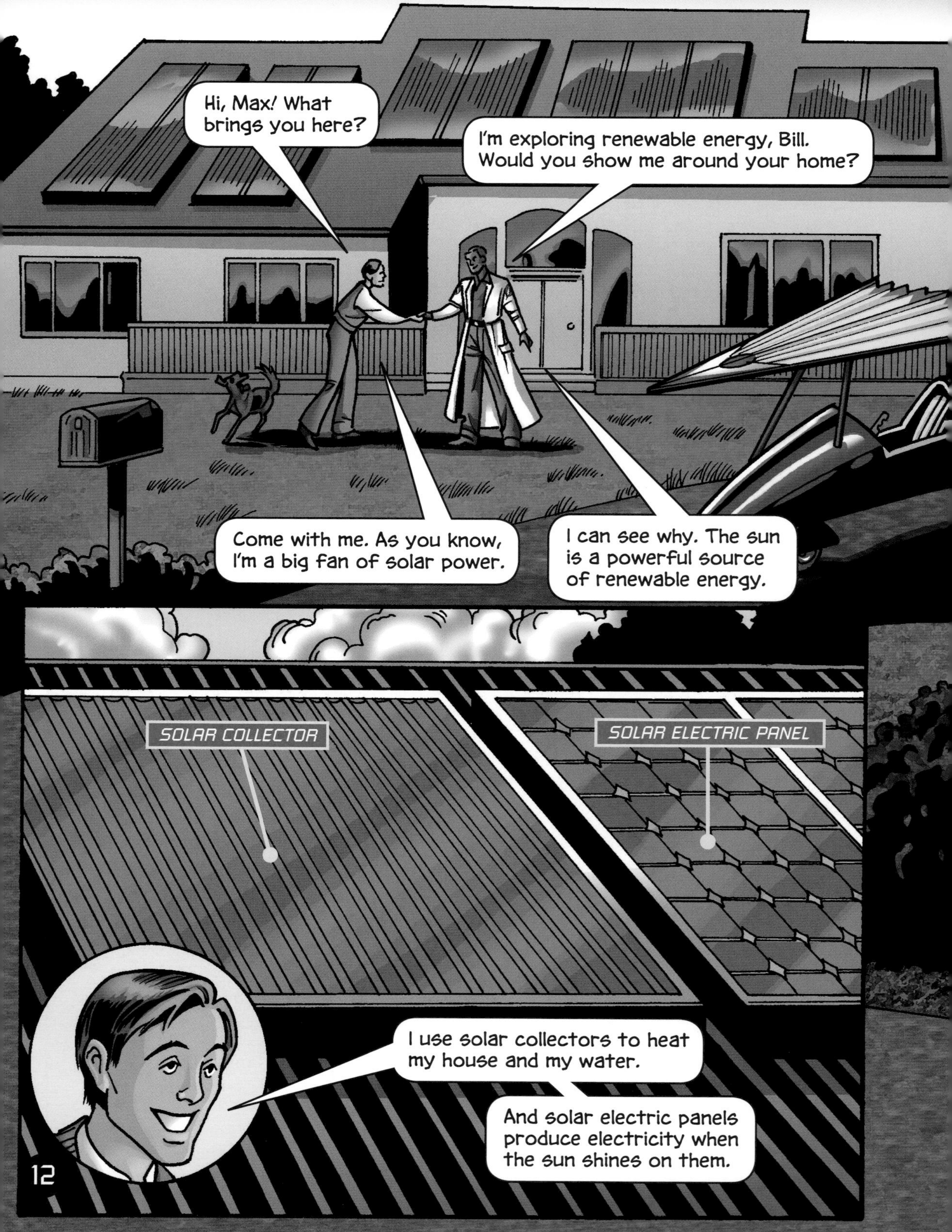
Hi, Max! What brings you here?
I'm exploring renewable energy, Bill. Would you show me around your home?
Come with me. As you know, I'm a big fan of solar power.
I can see why. The sun is a powerful source of renewable energy.
SOLAR COLLECTOR
SOLAR ELECTRIC PANEL
I use solar collectors to heat my house and my water.
And solar electric panels produce electricity when the sun shines on them.

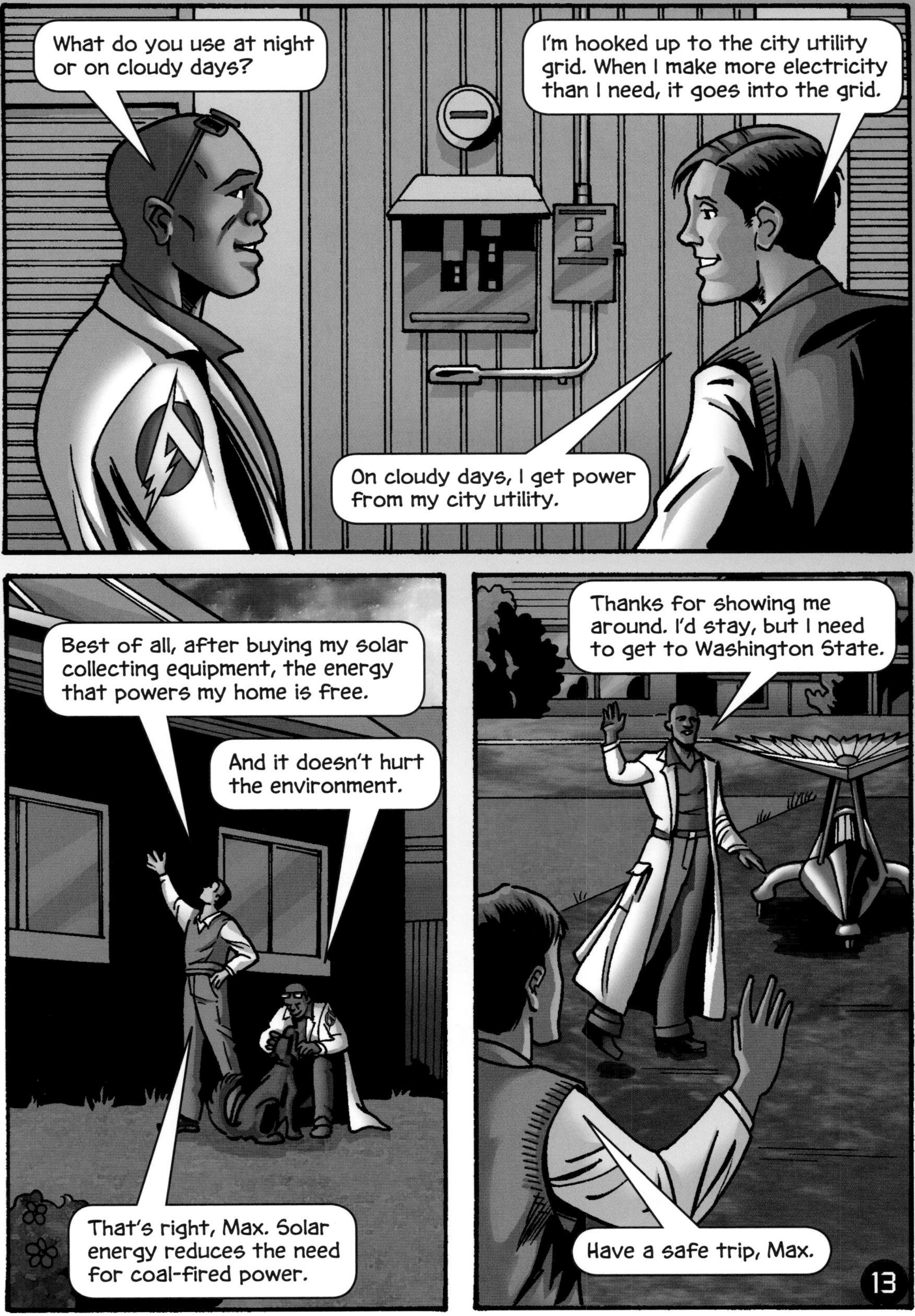
What do you use at night or on cloudy days?
I'm hooked up to the city utility grid. When I make more electricity than I need, it goes into the grid.
On cloudy days, I get power from my city utility.
Best of all, after buying my solar collecting equipment, the energy that powers my home is free.
And it doesn't hurt the environment.
That's right, Max. Solar energy reduces the need for coal-fired power.
Thanks for showing me around. I'd stay, but I need to get to Washington State.
Have a safe trip, Max.

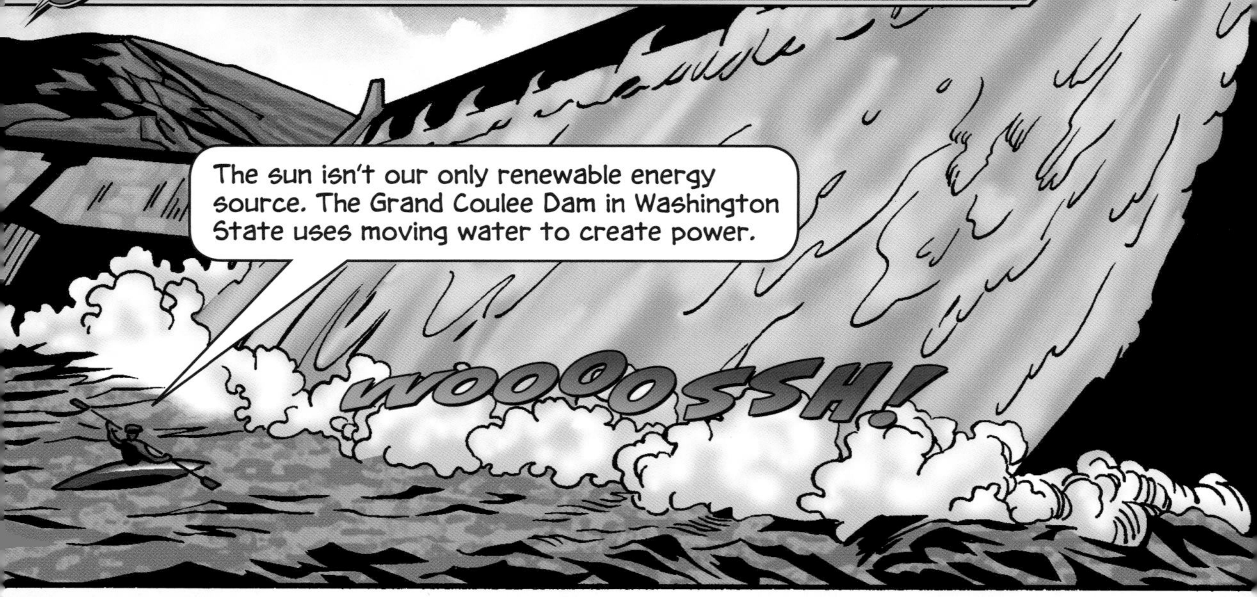
The sun isn't our only renewable energy source. The Grand Coulee Dam in Washington State uses moving water to create power.
WOOOOOSSH!

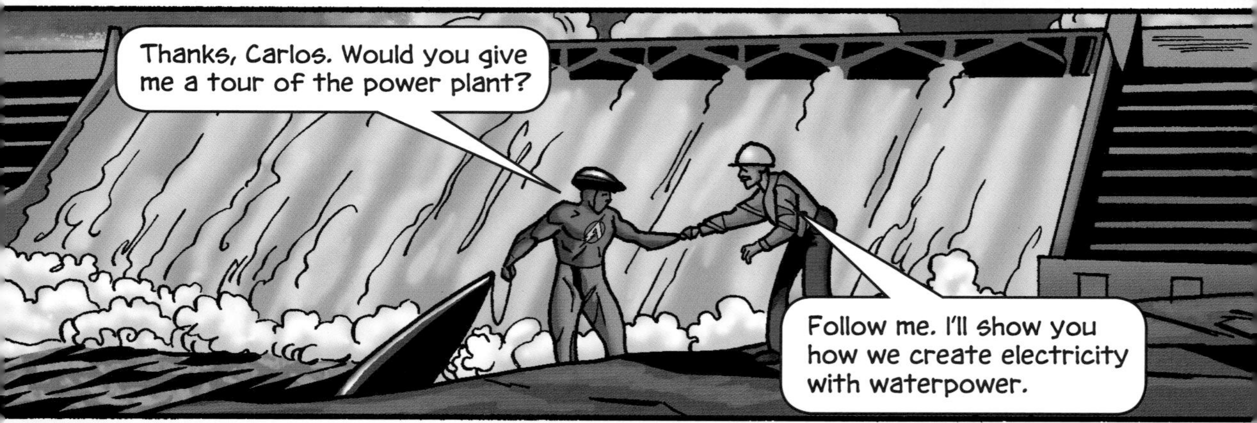
Thanks, Carlos. Would you give me a tour of the power plant?
Follow me. I'll show you how we create electricity with waterpower.

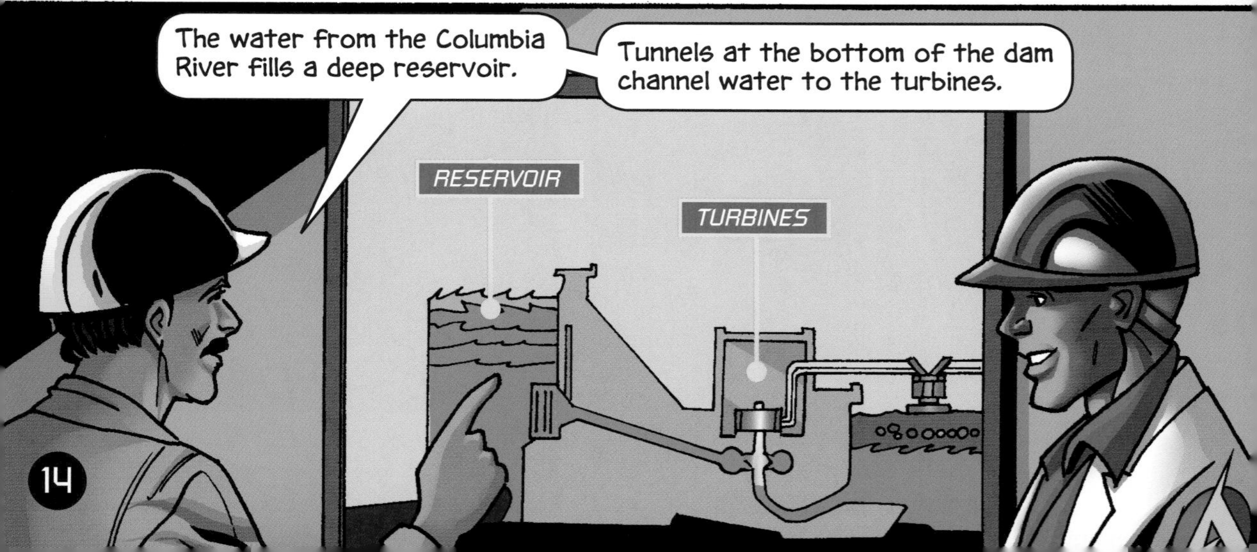
The water from the Columbia River fills a deep reservoir.
Tunnels at the bottom of the dam channel water to the turbines.
RESERVOIR
TURBINES

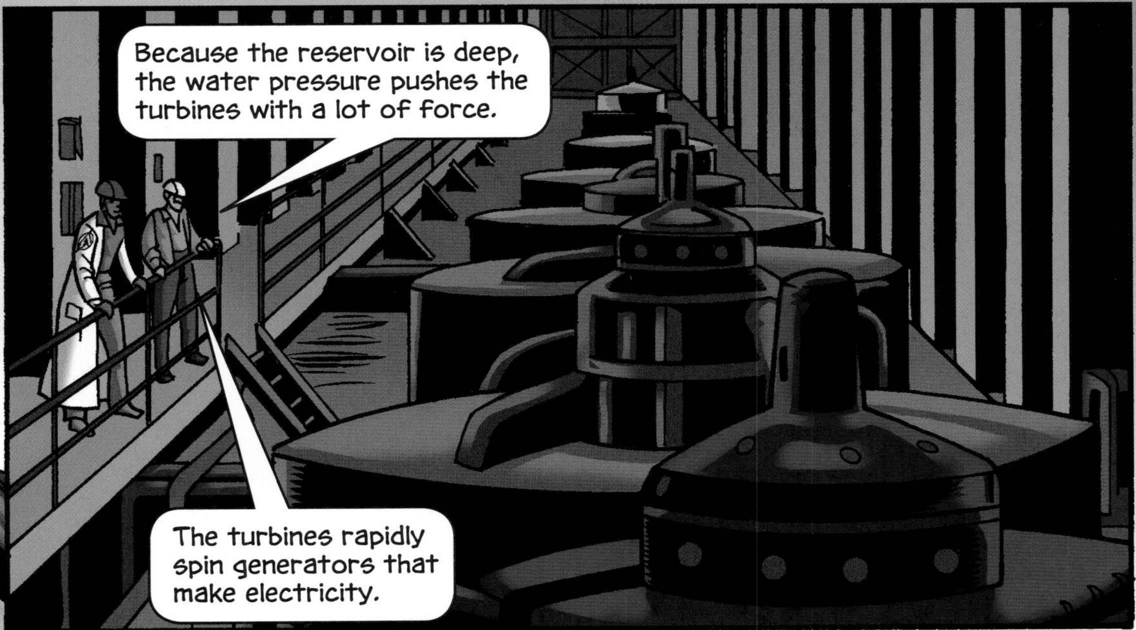
Because the reservoir is deep, the water pressure pushes the turbines with a lot of force.
The turbines rapidly spin generators that make electricity.

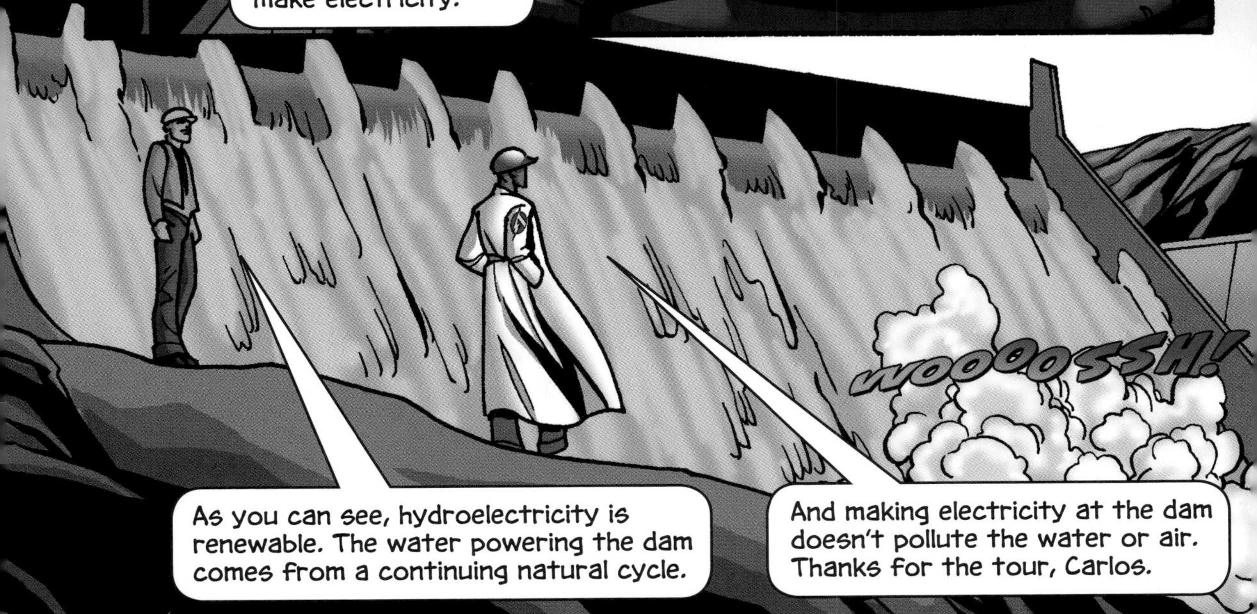
WOOOOOSSH!
As you can see, hydroelectricity is renewable. The water powering the dam comes from a continuing natural cycle.
And making electricity at the dam doesn't pollute the water or air. Thanks for the tour, Carlos.

HYDROELECTRIC HARM?

ACCESS GRANTED: MAX AXIOM

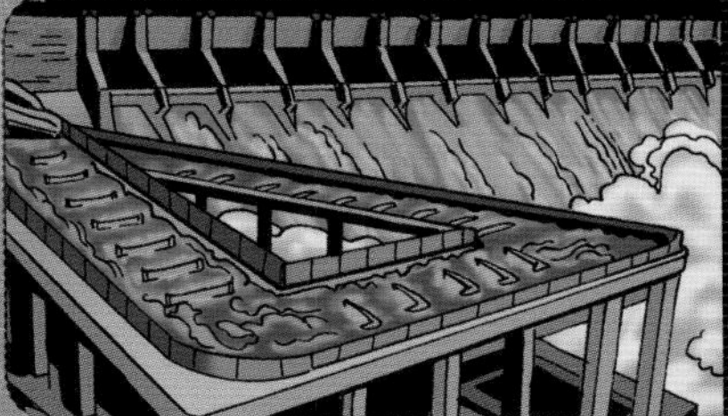

Hydroelectric power has some downsides. For instance, a dam's reservoir floods a large area. Wildlife in the area have to find somewhere else to live. Hydroelectric dams can also hurt fish. Fish can get caught in the dam and killed. Some newer dams have "fish ladders." These passageways help fish travel through the dam.

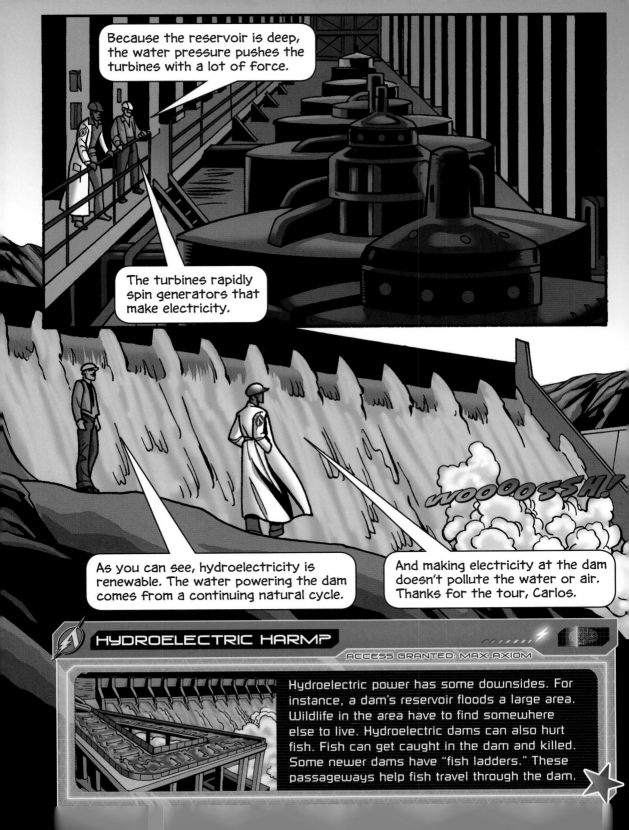

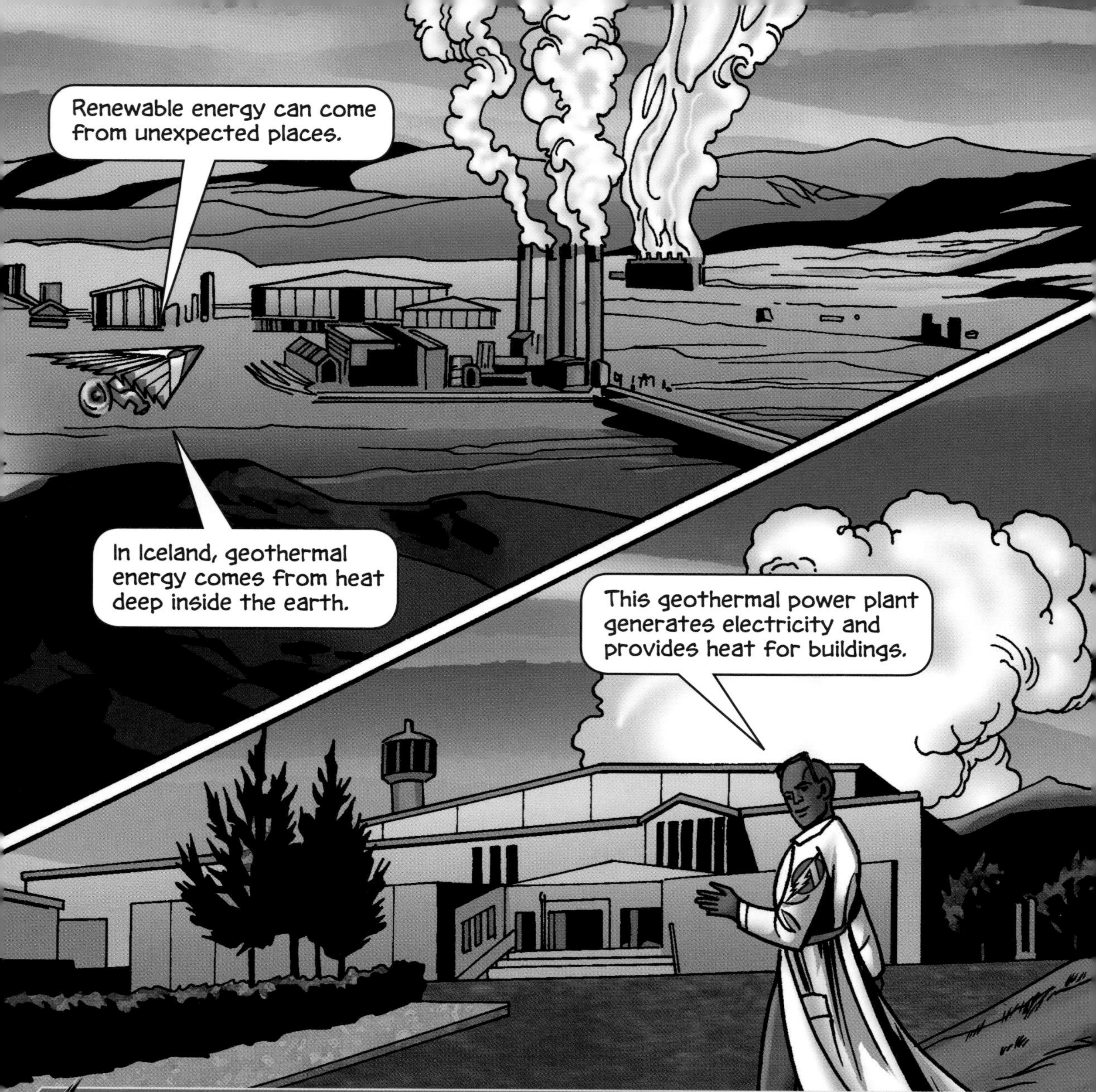
Renewable energy can come from unexpected places.
In Iceland, geothermal energy comes from heat deep inside the earth.
This geothermal power plant generates electricity and provides heat for buildings.

GEOTHERMAL POWER PLANTS

ACCESS GRANTED: MAX AXIOM

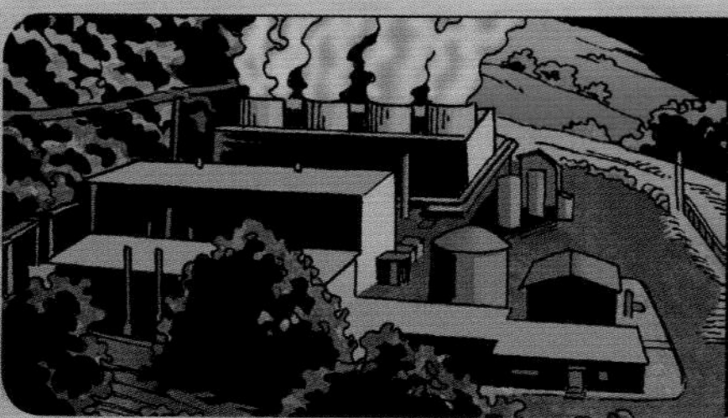

Geothermal power plants are found in more than 20 countries. In the United States, most geothermal power plants are found in Alaska, Hawaii, and states on the West Coast. The Geysers, the largest group of geothermal power plants in the world, is in California.

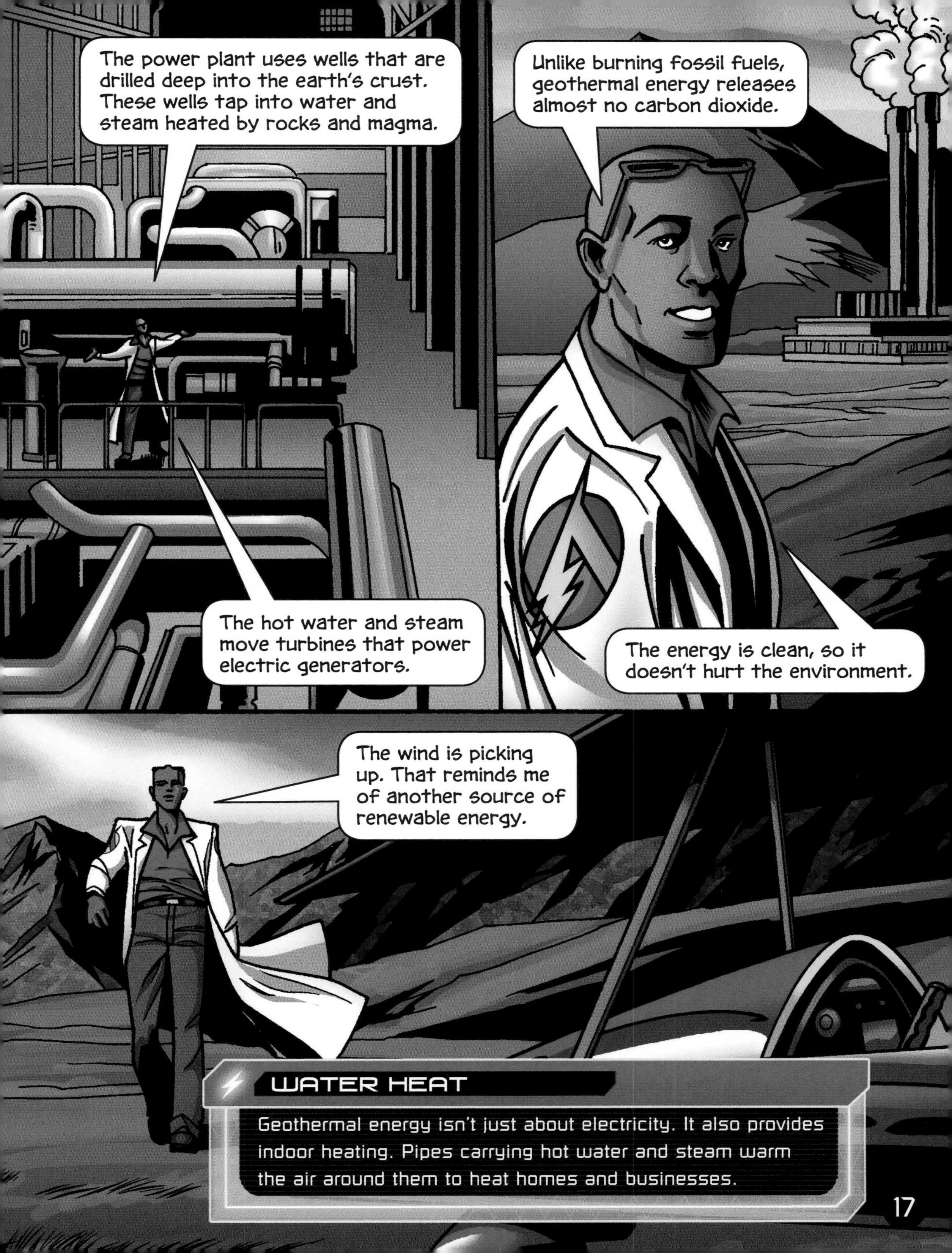
The power plant uses wells that are drilled deep into the earth's crust. These wells tap into water and steam heated by rocks and magma.
The hot water and steam move turbines that power electric generators.
Unlike burning fossil fuels, geothermal energy releases almost no carbon dioxide.
The energy is clean, so it doesn't hurt the environment.
The wind is picking up. That reminds me of another source of renewable energy.

WATER HEAT

Geothermal energy isn't just about electricity. It also provides indoor heating. Pipes carrying hot water and steam warm the air around them to heat homes and businesses.

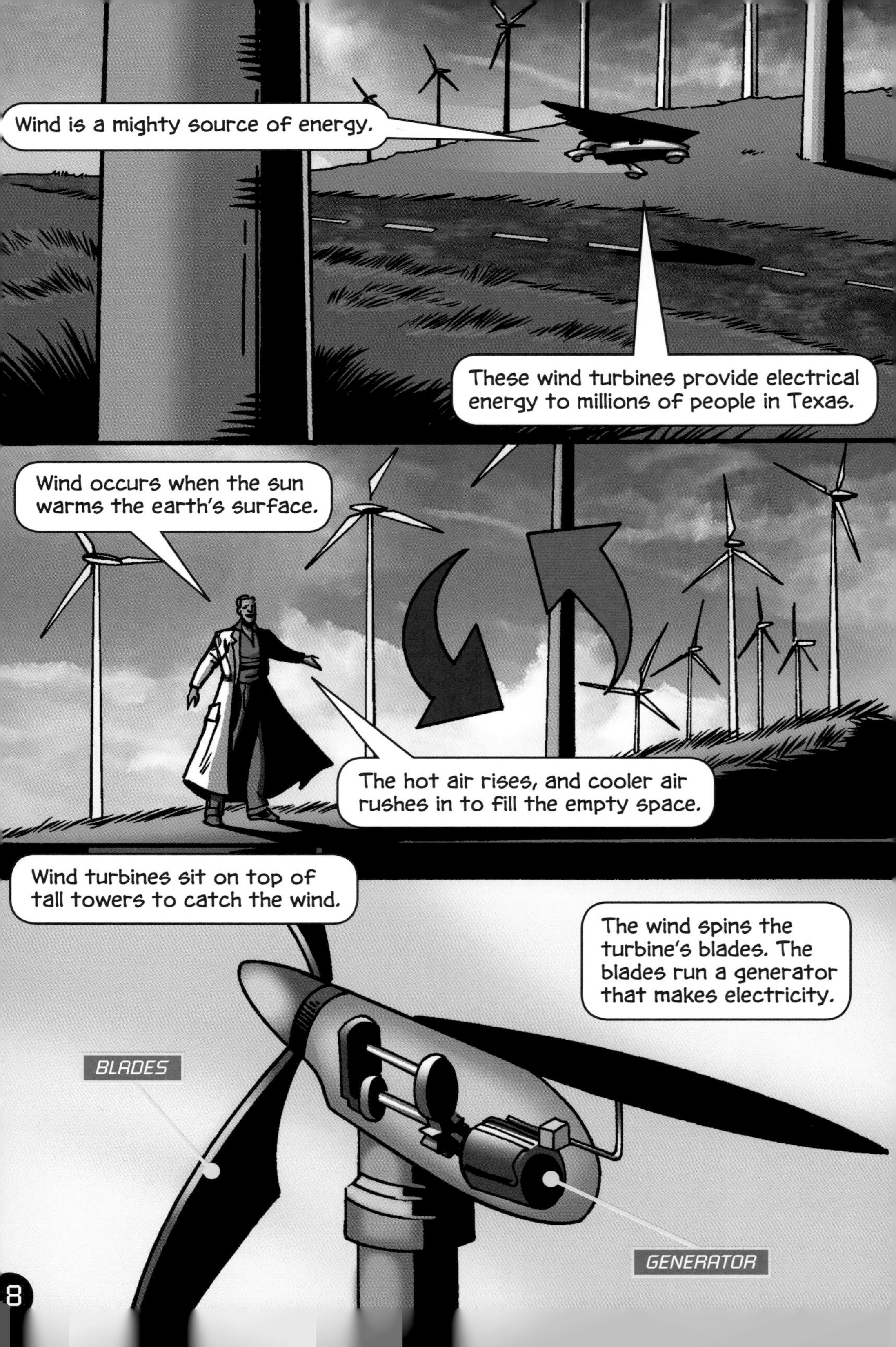
Wind is a mighty source of energy.
These wind turbines provide electrical energy to millions of people in Texas.
Wind occurs when the sun warms the earth's surface.
The hot air rises, and cooler air rushes in to fill the empty space.
Wind turbines sit on top of tall towers to catch the wind.
The wind spins the turbine's blades. The blades run a generator that makes electricity.
BLADES
GENERATOR

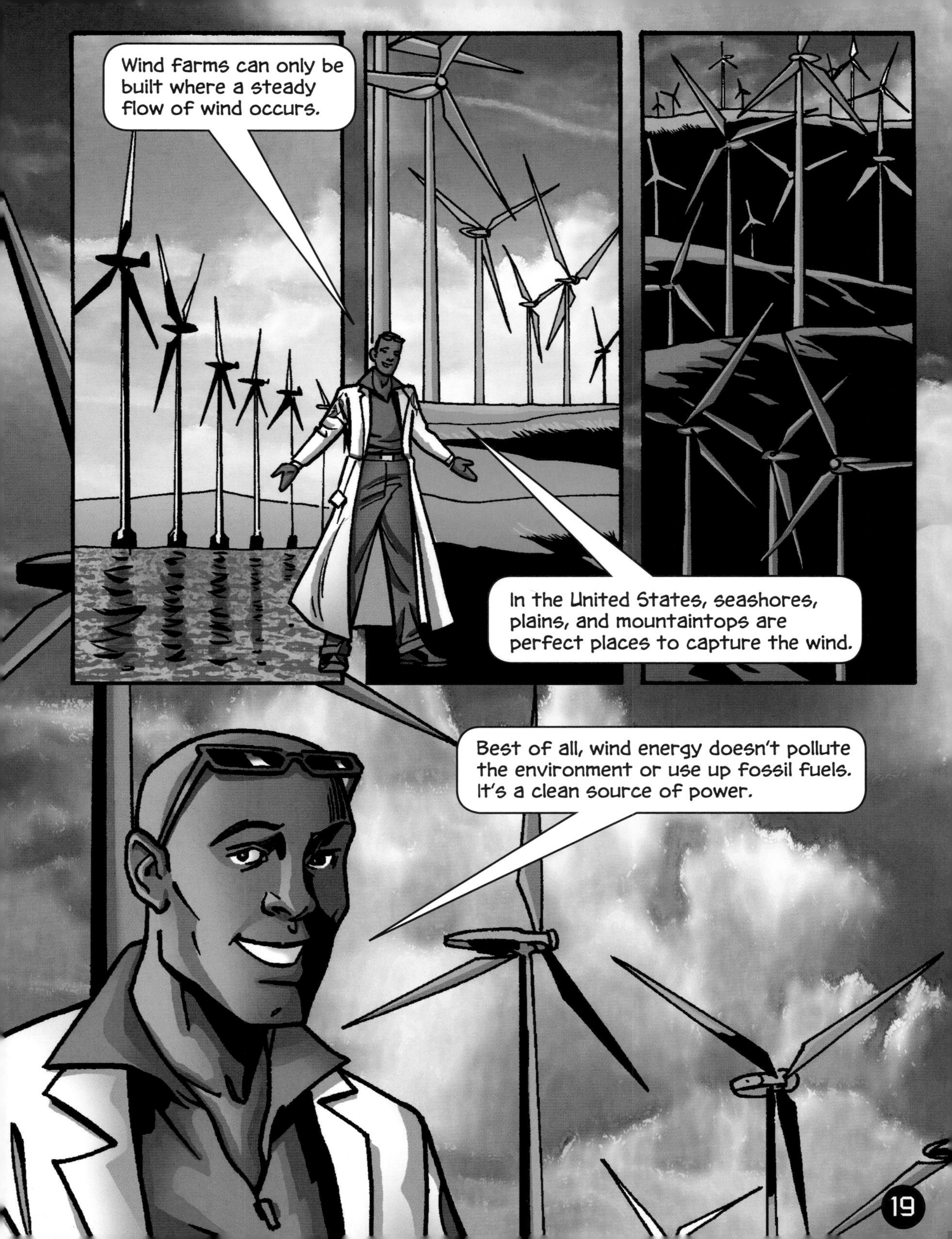
Wind farms can only be built where a steady flow of wind occurs.
In the United States, seashores, plains, and mountaintops are perfect places to capture the wind.
Best of all, wind energy doesn't pollute the environment or use up fossil fuels. It's a clean source of power.

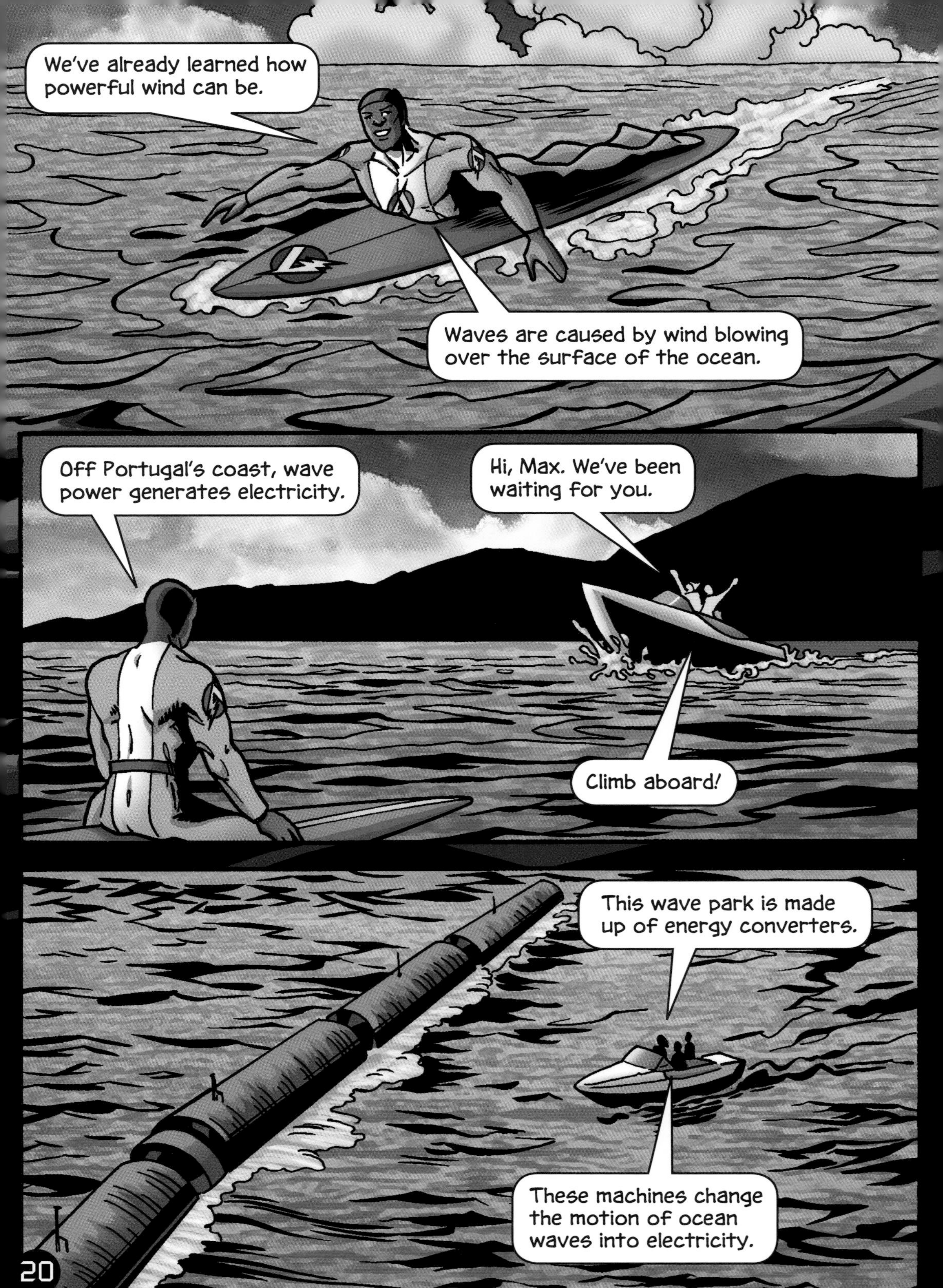
We've already learned how powerful wind can be.
Waves are caused by wind blowing over the surface of the ocean.
Off Portugal's coast, wave power generates electricity.
Hi, Max. We've been waiting for you.
Climb aboard!
This wave park is made up of energy converters.
These machines change the motion of ocean waves into electricity.

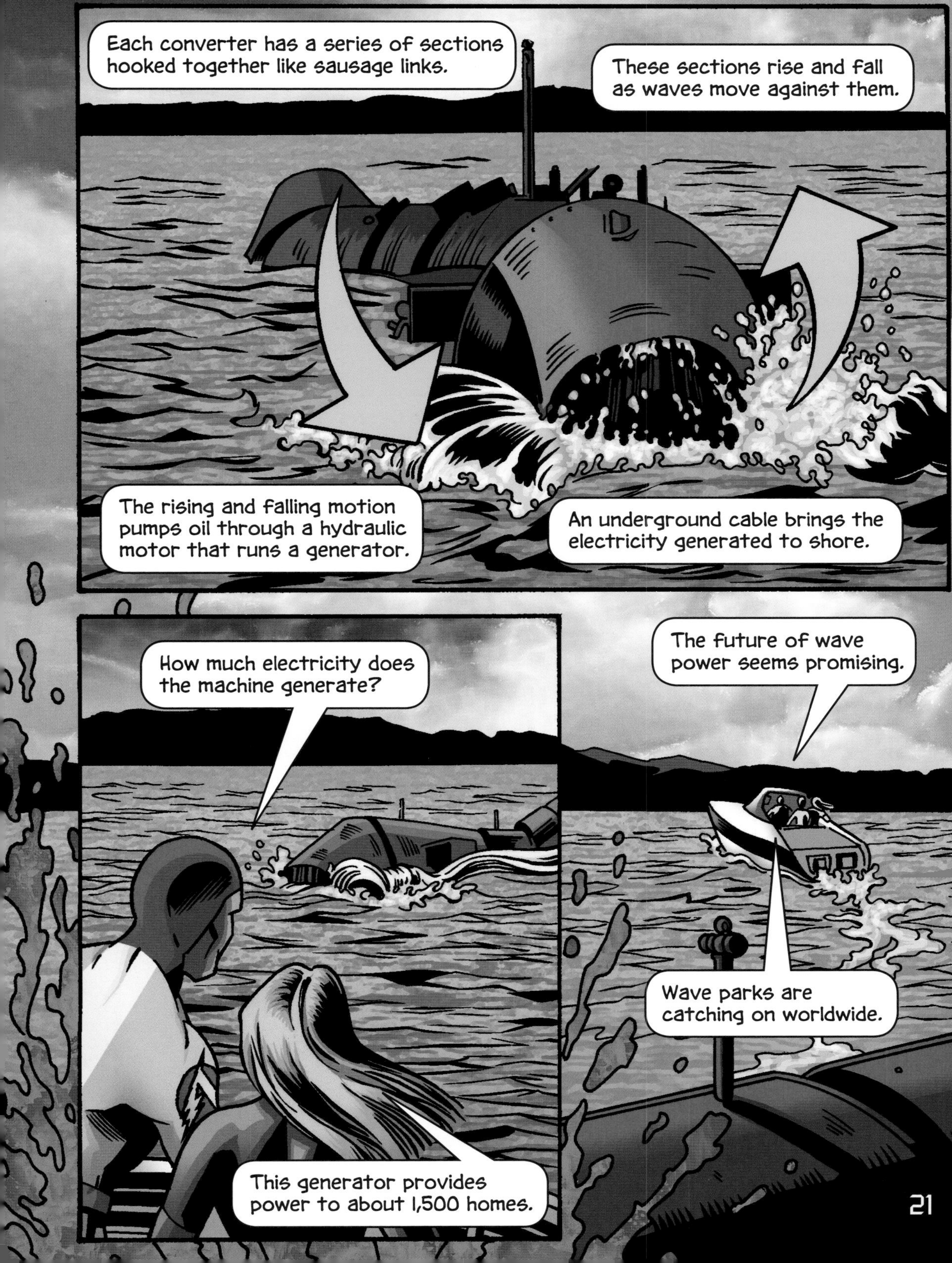
Each converter has a series of sections hooked together like sausage links.
These sections rise and fall as waves move against them.
The rising and falling motion pumps oil through a hydraulic motor that runs a generator.
An underground cable brings the electricity generated to shore.
How much electricity does the machine generate?
This generator provides power to about 1,500 homes.
The future of wave power seems promising.
Wave parks are catching on worldwide.

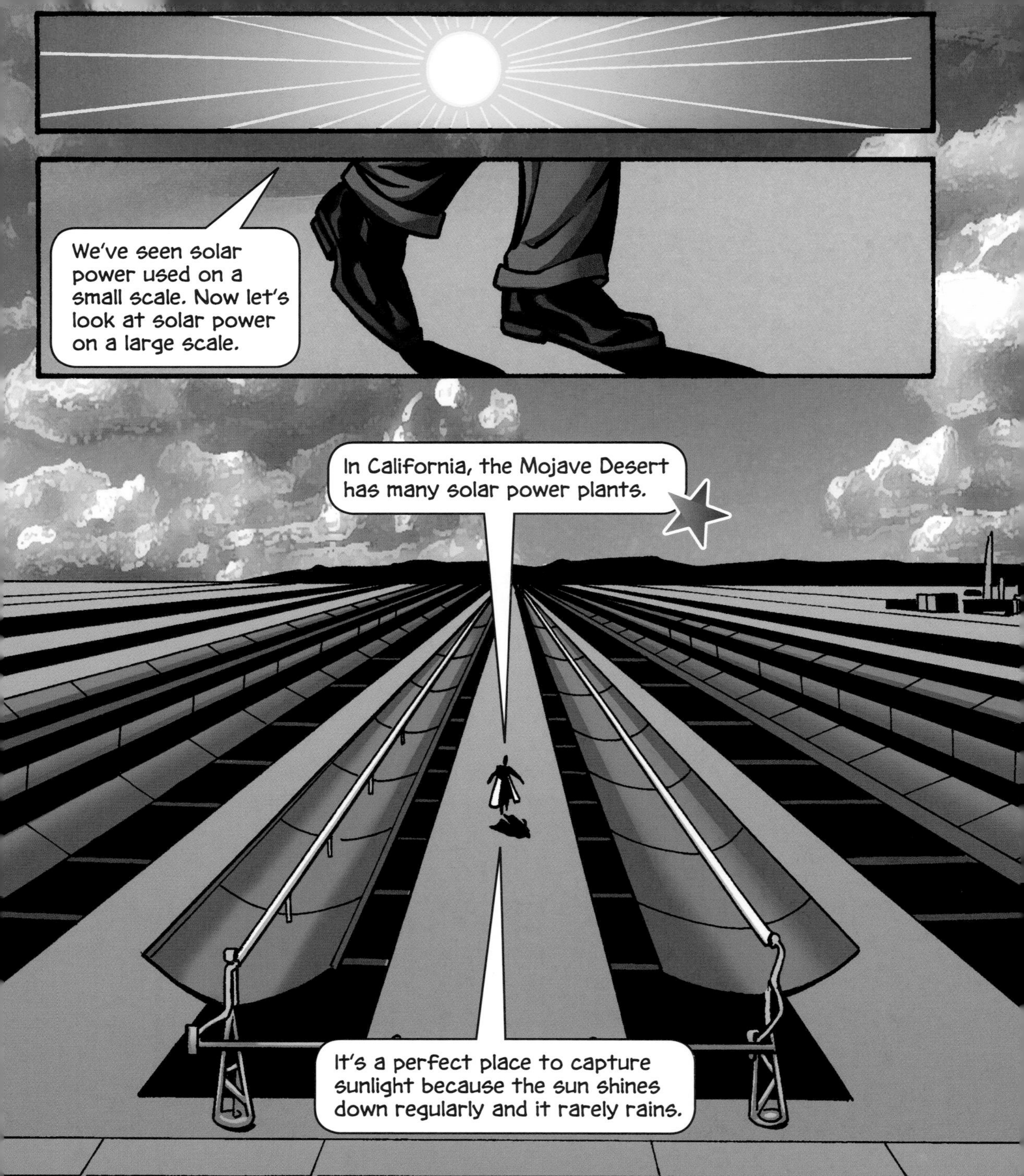
We've seen solar power used on a small scale. Now let's look at solar power on a large scale.
In California, the Mojave Desert has many solar power plants.
It's a perfect place to capture sunlight because the sun shines down regularly and it rarely rains.

POWER FROM SPACE

Scientists are working on new ways to use solar panels in space. The panels would change solar energy into a wavelength known as a microwave. These energy waves would be beamed to earth and changed into electricity.

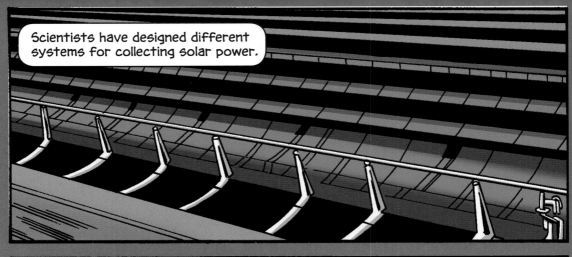

Scientists have designed different systems for collecting solar power.

This solar power plant uses curved mirrors to reflect sunlight onto a pipe filled with oil.

PIPE

The pipe carries the oil to heat exchangers. The hot oil heats water into steam. The steam turns turbines in a generator to make electricity. This solar power plant provides energy to thousands of homes.

The future of solar power is exciting. Let's find out about other new developments in renewable energy.

23

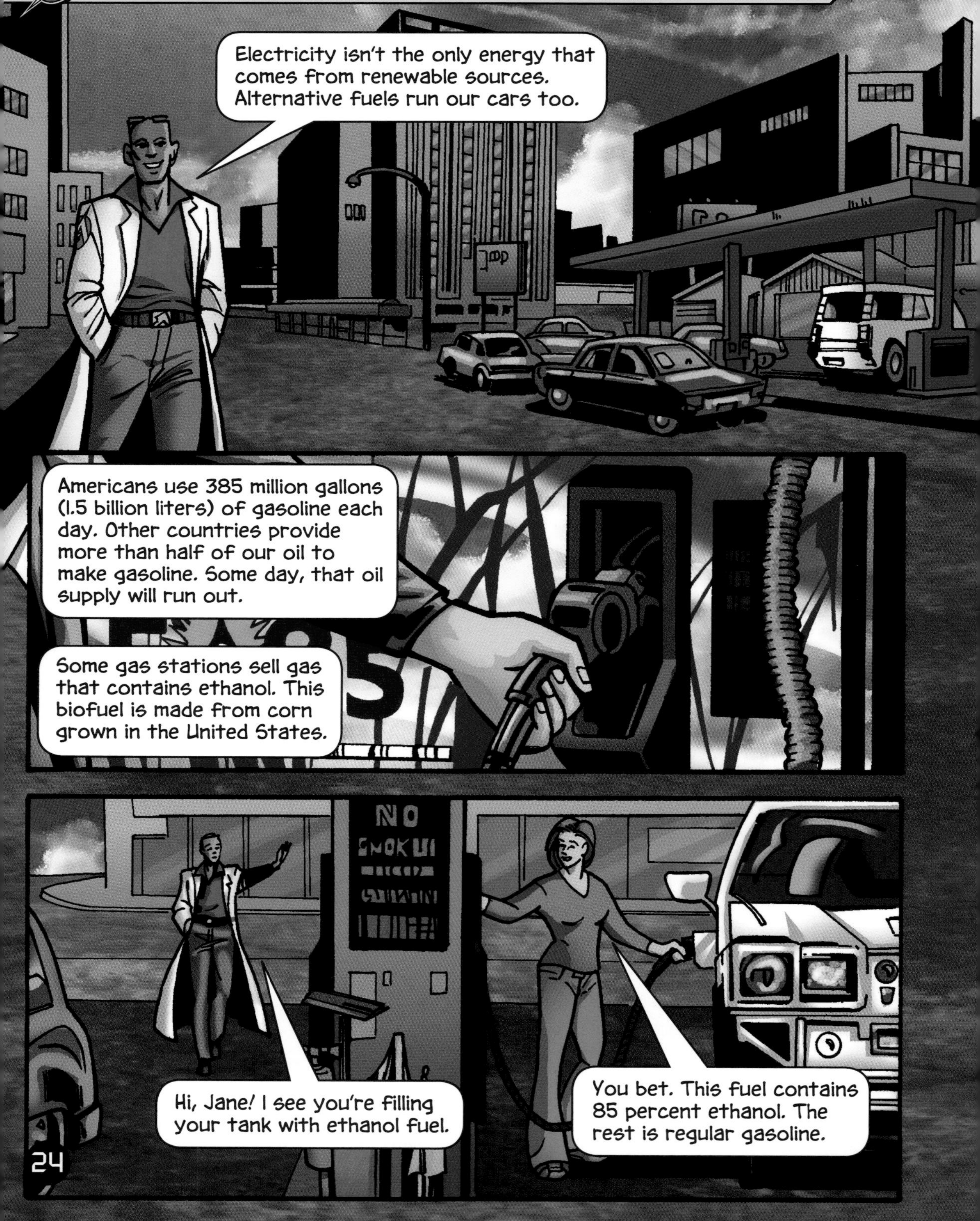

Electricity isn't the only energy that comes from renewable sources. Alternative fuels run our cars too.
Americans use 385 million gallons (1.5 billion liters) of gasoline each day. Other countries provide more than half of our oil to make gasoline. Some day, that oil supply will run out.
Some gas stations sell gas that contains ethanol. This biofuel is made from corn grown in the United States.
NO
Hi, Jane! I see you're filling your tank with ethanol fuel.
You bet. This fuel contains 85 percent ethanol. The rest is regular gasoline.

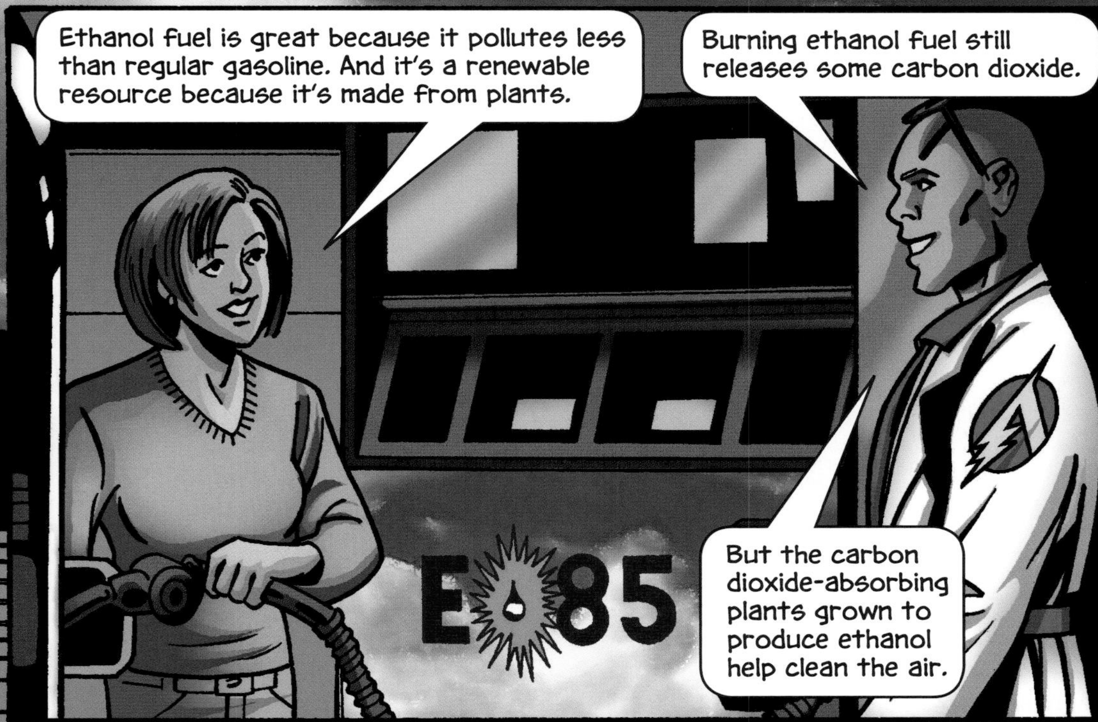
Ethanol fuel is great because it pollutes less than regular gasoline. And it's a renewable resource because it's made from plants.
Burning ethanol fuel still releases some carbon dioxide.
E85
But the carbon dioxide-absorbing plants grown to produce ethanol help clean the air.

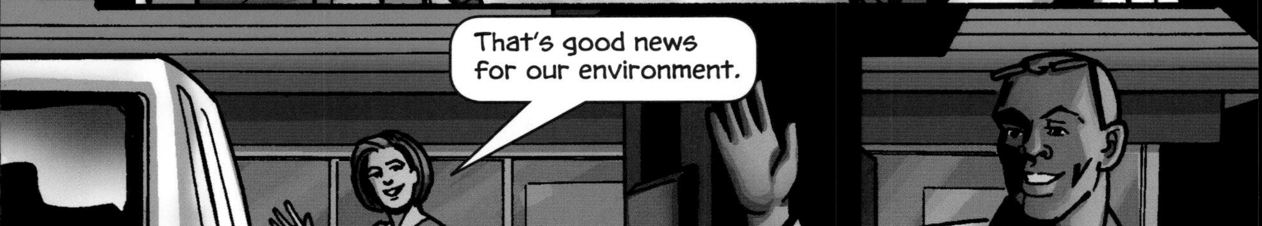
That's good news for our environment.
Thanks for doing your part to keep it clean, Jane. Have a good trip.

FOOD OR FUEL?

ACCESS GRANTED: MAX AXIOM

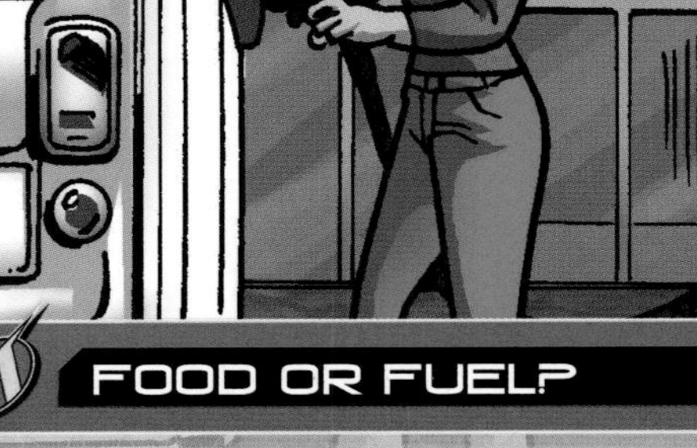

One downside of ethanol fuel is that it uses crops for transportation instead of food. Scientists want to take the biofuel burden off of our food supply. They are working on ways to make biofuel from nonfood plants and crop waste.

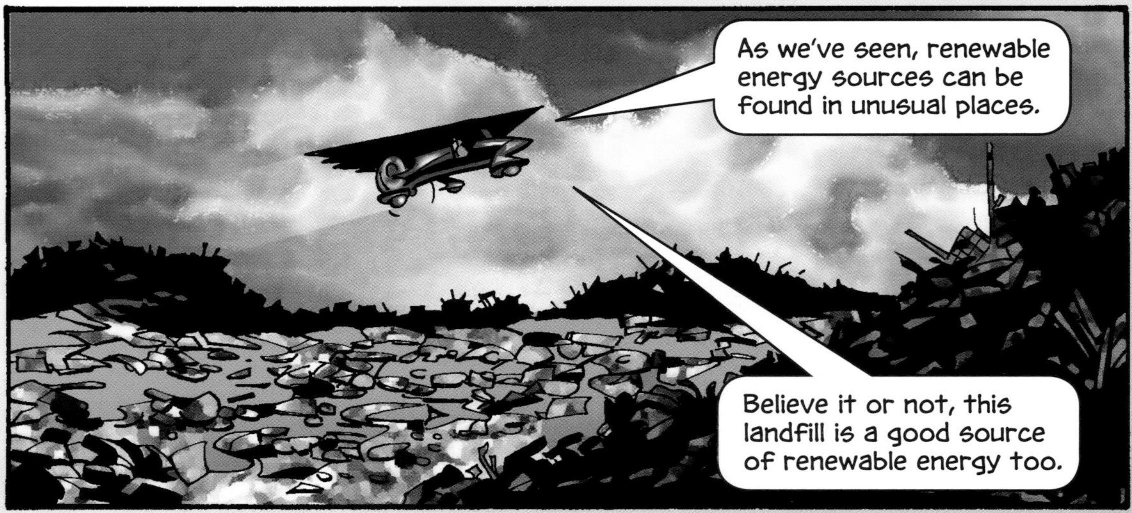
As we've seen, renewable energy sources can be found in unusual places.
Believe it or not, this landfill is a good source of renewable energy too.

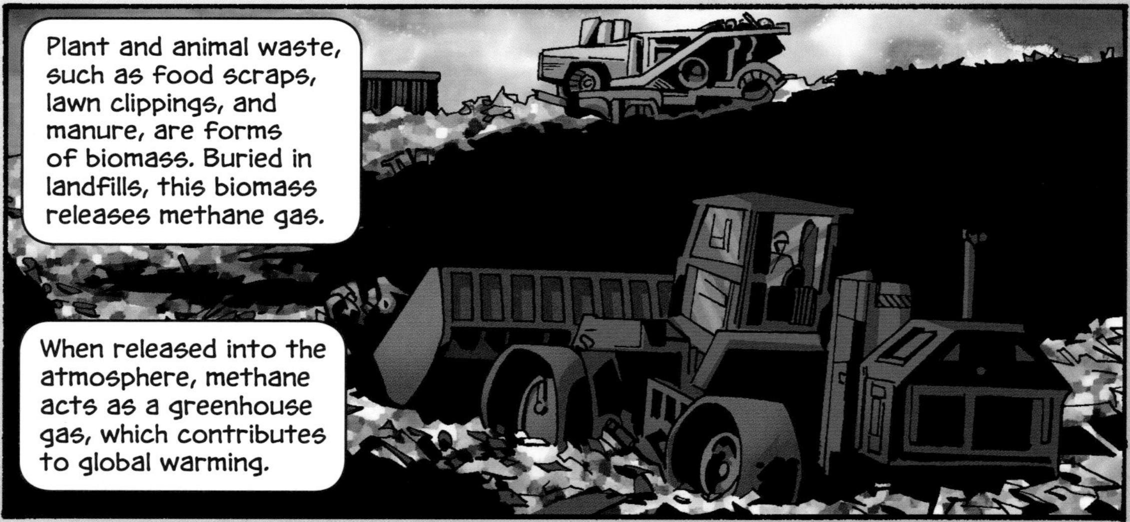
Plant and animal waste, such as food scraps, lawn clippings, and manure, are forms of biomass. Buried in landfills, this biomass releases methane gas.
When released into the atmosphere, methane acts as a greenhouse gas, which contributes to global warming.

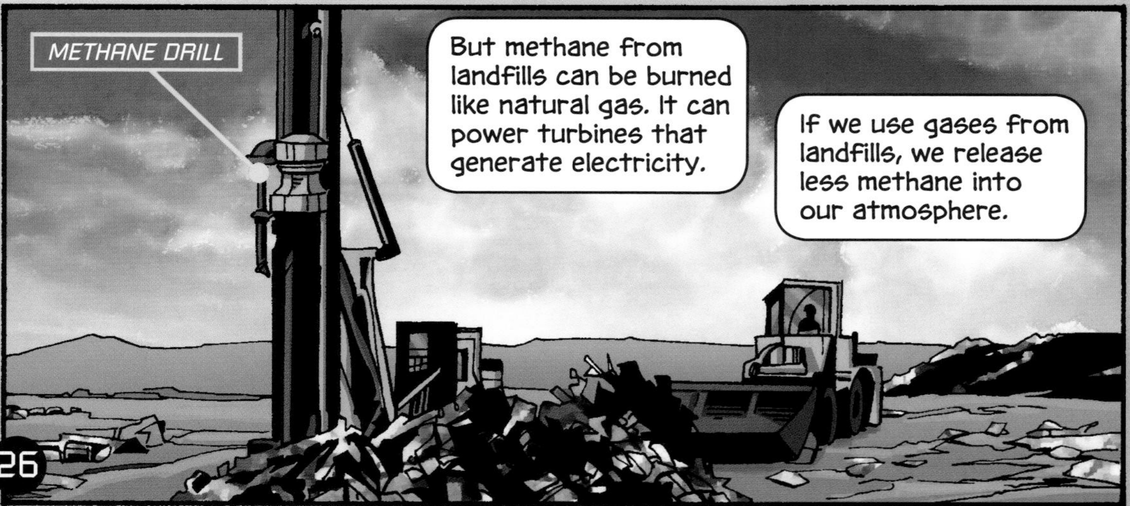
METHANE DRILL
But methane from landfills can be burned like natural gas. It can power turbines that generate electricity.
If we use gases from landfills, we release less methane into our atmosphere.

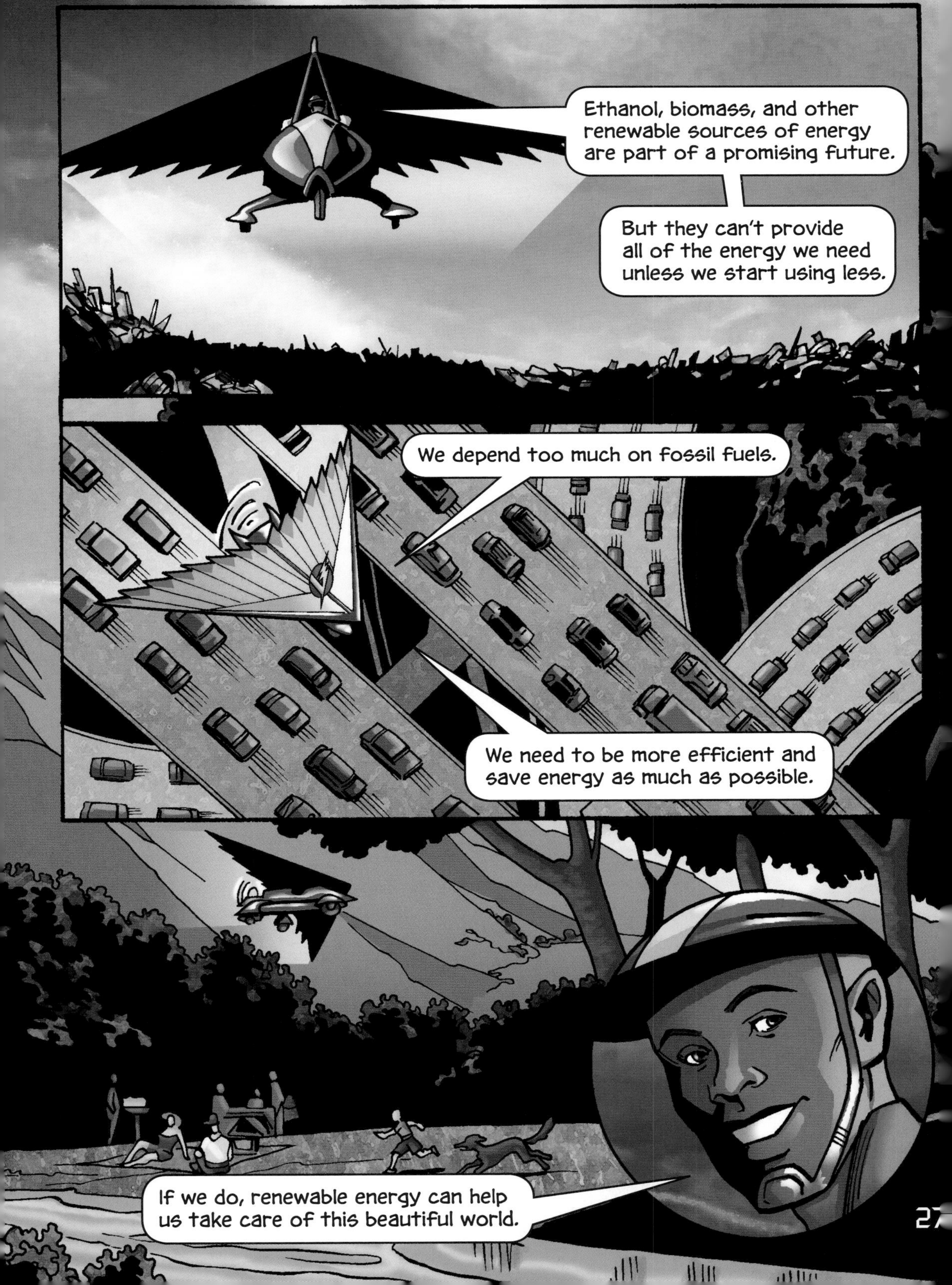
Ethanol, biomass, and other renewable sources of energy are part of a promising future.
But they can't provide all of the energy we need unless we start using less.
We depend too much on fossil fuels.
We need to be more efficient and save energy as much as possible.
If we do, renewable energy can help us take care of this beautiful world.

MORE ABOUT
RENEWABLE ENERGY

Hydroelectricity is the most widely used form of renewable energy. In the United States, about 7 percent of electrical power comes from hydroelectricity.

Capturing energy from the sun is not a new idea. In the 1500s, artist and inventor Leonardo da Vinci sketched plans for using solar energy to heat water.

Only about 1 percent of the United States' electricity comes from wind power. Scientists estimate that by 2030, nearly 20 percent of U.S. energy will come from wind.

Researchers are working on putting solar farms on the ocean. But some scientists believe that solar panels on the ocean would block sunlight and upset the ocean's animal and plant life.

Almost all of Iceland's electricity comes from geothermal and hydroelectric energy sources. Most of Iceland's homes are heated with geothermal energy.

Scientists have found a way to make biofuel from algae. Algae is easy to grow and takes up less space than land crops like corn or soybeans.

In 1896, inventor Henry Ford designed his first car to run on 100 percent ethanol fuel.

A fuel cell is like a battery. It converts chemical energy into electricity. Today, fuel cells are an experimental source of power in some buildings. Automakers are developing cars that use hydrogen fuel cells. These cars use hydrogen fuel, instead of gasoline or diesel fuel, to run an electric motor.

Used vegetable oil from fast food restaurants doesn't have to go to waste. It can be recycled to power cars. The vegetable oil is combined with ingredients such as lye and methanol to make biofuel. This "fast food fuel" works great—and it smells like french fries!

WATER-POWERED WINCH

Moving water is a powerful form of renewable energy. See that power in action with this winch!

WHAT YOU NEED:

- ruler
- empty 2-liter bottle
- marker
- utility knife
- 2 small binder clips
- 2 thin plastic container lids
- scissors
- chopstick
- 12-inch (30-cm) piece of string
- tape
- small toy
- pitcher
- water

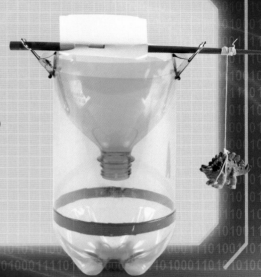

WHAT YOU DO:

1. Measure 7 inches (18 centimeters) up from the bottom of the 2-liter bottle. Using a marker, draw a line around the bottle at this height.

2. Ask an adult to carefully cut along the line with the utility knife to remove the top of the bottle.

3. Place the bottle top upside down inside the bottom of the bottle. Clip two binder clips on opposite edges of the bottle top. Flip the inside handles of the binder clips down.

4. Measure and cut two 2 ¾-inch by 3-inch (70-millimeter by 76-mm) rectangles from the centers of plastic lids.

5. Fold one piece of plastic in half along the short side.

6. Measure and mark lines every ½ inch (13 mm) along the folded edge.

7. Use a pair of scissors to cut short slits at each mark.

8. Repeat steps 5 through 7 with the other plastic piece.

9. Unfold the rectangles and place them back to back so their slits line up. Weave the chopstick through the slits in both pieces of plastic to hold them together. Spread the four plastic flaps apart to create a water wheel.

10. Tie and tape the string to the longer side of the chopstick. Tie the end of the string string around the toy.

11. Gently pour water onto the center of one of the paddles to turn the winch. As the winch turns it will lift the toy.

DISCUSSION QUESTIONS

1. Which two renewable resources discussed in the book do you think could be used in your area? Explain why you think so.

2. Methane is sometimes produced by waste materials in landfills. Do you think using methane from biomass would have helpful or hurtful effects on the environment?

3. Max discusses several kinds of renewable energy. Which one do you think has the most positive impact on the environment and why?

4. Some people have solar panels on their rooftops to power their homes. What are some advantages and disadvantages of solar energy?

WRITING PROMPTS

1. In your own words, write definitions for renewable and nonrenewable energy. Then list examples of each.

2. Imagine that your local community is deciding on a new form of renewable energy to install. Write a letter to the editor in support of the form of renewable energy you like best while also explaining its benefits.

3. Think about solar energy and wind energy, two forms of renewable energy. Write a short essay comparing and contrasting them, and defend the one you think is best for the environment.

4. Engineers designed fish ladders to help fish travel upstream past hydroelectric dams. Imagine you need to design a new system for fish to get around dams. Write a short paragraph explaining how your system would work and then draw a picture of it.

TAKE A QUIZ!

biofuel (BYE-oh-fyoo-uhl)—a fuel made of, or produced from, plant material

biomass (BYE-oh-mass)—plant materials and animal waste used as a source of fuel

crust (KRUHST)—the thin outer layer of earth's surface

ethanol (ETH-uh-nal)—a biofuel made from crops such as corn and sugarcane

fossil fuels (FOSS-uhl FYOO-uhls)—natural fuels formed from the remains of plants and animals; coal, oil, and natural gas are fossil fuels.

generator (JEN-uh-ray-tur)—a machine that makes electricity by turning a magnet inside a coil of wire

geothermal (jee-oh-THUR-muhl)—relating to the intense heat inside the earth

hydraulic (hye-DRAW-lik)—having to do with a system powered by fluid forced through pipes or chambers

hydroelectricity (hye-droh-i-lek-TRISS-uh-tee)—a form of energy caused by flowing water

microwave (MYE-kroh-wave)—a wavelength in the electromagnetic spectrum

reservoir (REZ-ur-vwar)—a holding area for large amounts of water or steam

turbine (TUR-bine)—an engine powered by steam or gas

READ MORE

Brundle, Harriet. *Renewable Energy.* Climate Change: Our Impact on Earth. Farmington Hills, MI: Greenhaven Publishing, 2018.

Dickmann, Nancy. *Using Renewable Energy.* Putting the Planet First. New York, NY: Crabtree Publishing, 2018.

Labrecuqe, Ellen. *Renewable Energy.* North Mankato, MN: Cherry Lake Publishing, 2017.

INTERNET SITES

Energy Information Administration: Energy Kids - Renewable Energy
https://www.eia.gov/kids/energy.php?page=renewable_home-basics

National Geographic: Renewable Energy
https://www.nationalgeographic.org/encyclopedia/renewable-energy/

Greenchild: 8 Awesome Facts About Renewable Energy
https://www.greenchildmagazine.com/8-awesome-facts-about-renewable-energy/

Super-cool stuff!

Check out projects, games, and lots more at
www.capstonekids.com

INDEX